China Dispatches:
20 Short Stories From a Society in Transformation

Hatty Liu

First published in 2022 by Royal Collins Publishing Group Inc.
Groupe Publication Royal Collins Inc.
BKM Royalcollins Publishers Private Limited

Headquarters: 550-555 boul. René-Lévesque O Montréal (Québec) H2Z1B1 Canada
India office: 805 Hemkunt House, 8th Floor, Rajendra Place, New Delhi 110 008

Original Edition © The World of Chinese Magazine
The Commercial Press

ISBN: 978-1-4878-0861-7

To find out more about our publications, please visit www.royalcollins.com.

T0002682

Contents

Foreword

"We tell ourselves stories in order to live," writer Joan Didion declared at the dawn of the American New Journalism movement in 1968. It is with the intention of making contemporary China come alive in narratives that The World of Chinese (TWOC) magazine presents this anthology.

Published six times a year in English by The Commercial Press since 2006, TWOC is a magazine with a mission. Under the slogan "Sharing stories, sharing culture," and later, "China is a story—we tell it," the award-winning magazine has developed a reputation for conscientious reporting, sharp cultural criticism, and some of the best quality narrative journalism on China in the English language.

The chapters in this inaugural anthology first appeared as stand-alone features, profiles, and cultural analyses in the 2015 to 2019 issues of the magazine, and were selected for their ability to reflect a spectrum of contemporary concerns in Chinese society. These stories vary widely in tone and subject matter, ranging from lighthearted debates about Chinese desserts to clear-eyed inquiries into equality, justice, and the consequences of economic development.

They share, though, TWOC's commitment to fresh takes and human angles. Each TWOC feature is reported with extensive fact-checking, notes on relevant historical, cultural, and linguistic contexts, and first-hand quotations and viewpoints gathered by writers who have traveled to—even lived within—the communities affected. The characters featured in these pages are mostly ordinary; not always heroic; and often bewildered by the pace of changes around them. Their voices often fall by the wayside of new cycles concerned with economic triumphs and global power plays—yet their experiences contribute important human nuances to how Chinese society is evolving today, and the directions it will take in the future.

In the meanwhile, they will just live.

Chapter One: Fashion

"New clothes are always the best,
but old people are always the better."

- Anonymous, "Gu Yan Ge"

Class Acts

For a century, school uniforms have mirrored social and political shifts in China

It's not unusual to hear complaints about mandatory school uniforms—least of all in China. In 2015 China Daily remarked that Chinese netizens felt their uniforms "could claim the global crown" in ugliness. The newspaper cited a Weibo survey in which just 10 percent of respondents said they looked good, while 44.6 percent were happy to call school uniforms ugly—slack, shapeless track suits with "no aesthetic value at all."

Scrapping uniforms altogether is an unlikely solution, though. While some deplore the homogeneity, others are loath to let personal appearance become a distraction. In March 2017, one school in Fujian had to ban imported sneakers, explaining that students were constantly one-upping each other with expensive footwear.

While schools such as the Zhengzhou Experimental School are beginning to explore clothing more clearly defined by gender, others are importing styles from the UK and South Korea. Schools have even hosted fashion shows to help improve the aesthetics of mandatory school attire.

But as inequality grows in society, uniforms are becoming yet another form of status symbol—then again, how students dress has always had important political and social implications in China.

Indeed, uniforms were first introduced in the fallout of the crippling defeat of the Second Opium War as part of an urgent call to learn from the West. Encouraged by missionaries, Qing officials sponsored numerous "new" schools in Beijing, Fuzhou and Shanghai in which foreign languages, science and military knowledge replaced Confucian texts. Clad in robes, hats, and boots, their students wore uniforms similar to the attire of government officials—albeit without the badges of rank—to show that their education was in the service of government (women were not allowed to enroll).

By the time of the Republic of China (1912 – 1949), alterations in apparel and customs became critical components of the government's larger social and political reforms. Besides abolishing the Manchu "queue" and female foot binding, the government stipulated that official ceremonial wear for men should be a black tuxedo with a silk hat. In the same year, the Ministry of Education stated that "male uniforms should resemble that of common military training wear," based on Western officer garb.

Students returning from Japan brought new features, including stand-up collars. Japanese-inspired suits, originally based on Prussian military designs, they were called "students' suits" (学生装) in China. But despite a newfound eagerness to modernize the nation through outside ideas, the Republic was also characterized

PHOTOGRAPH BY FOTOE

Chinese architect and poet Lin Huiyin (far right) and cousins in middle-school uniforms in 1916 by strong nationalistic sentiments; regulations expected that "school uniforms should be mainly made of plain, strong materials produced within the country."

Although restrictions had been lifted since 1907, female schools were rare and limited to students from elite families. They wore unembroidered versions of the era's typical female attire, usually a cropped cheongsam top and black skirt, a look known as the "civilized new outfit" (文明新装) which drew admiring commentary from some in the intellectual class. "Ever since the flourishing of female schools, all students wear light makeup and simple, elegant clothes," noted scholar Xu Ke, who deplored the bound feet, piercings, jewelry, and excessive makeup that had long epitomized female beauty standards. "Even women in brothels copy [their] look."

Nevertheless the May Fourth Movement—in which over 3,000 students gathered in front of the former Forbidden City to protest the terms of the Treaty of Versailles on May 4, 1919—stunned the establishment. Speaking with patriotic fervor and eloquence, the students demanded a modernizing nation that adopted ideas from Western civilization. The ensuing publicity cemented their attire within the national imagination, and women's uniforms became known as "May Fourth suits" (五四装); they are now ubiquitous in films and TV shows about the early Republican period.

Surprisingly, traditional Manchurian gowns made a comeback in the 1920s and 30s as women began favoring a single cheongsam over their previous two-piece outfits. "It is not to show loyalty to the Manchurian Qing government, advocating the restoration of the monarch, but because women are intentionally mimicking men," noted writer Eileen Chang. "Influenced by Western culture and infatuated with the idea of gender quality...

PHOTOGRAPH BY FOTOE

In the heady days of post-revolution diversity during the early 1950s, students on Heilongjiang University's campus wore a variety of individual styles

they reject all feminine qualities and would rather exterminate all characteristics of women. The early *qipao* were squared shaped and quite stern, bearing the air of the puritans." At schools, *qipao* were usually plain white or Indanthrene blue, but the newly fashionable cheongsam soon took society by storm, quickly evolving away from its prudish origins into tight fitting, revealing versions.

The war-torn 1940s ended with the arrival of the Communist government in 1949. Unlike their Republic predecessors, attire was probably the least priority for the Maoists, who were far more concerned with the notion of a united front between workers, peasants and intellectuals. In Yuan Ze and Hu Yue's *One Hundred Years of Clothing*, one Peking University student recalled a riot of clothing styles in these early years, including worker's gear, long gowns, *qipao*, Western suits and leather shoes.

It didn't last long. Amid a series of ideological campaigns, the drab, unadorned aesthetic of the worker and peasant classes became the dominant style, casting a long shadow on fashion that, in many schools, continues to this day. Yet this Marxist zeal gave rise to one particularly colorful item—the red scarf.

Symbolizing a corner of the Communist red flag—itself a symbol of the revolutionary martyrs' blood—the scarf is the symbol of the Young Pioneers, the preteen stepping-stone to the Communist Youth League. Inspired by Soviet style, Young Pioneers wore white shirts and dark trousers, or knee-length skirts for girls. After 1952, girls were allowed to wear floral skirts, because children were the "flowers of the nation," but as left-wing thought hardened in the 1960s, military styles became en vogue. Proud schoolboys would aspire to wear a blue-striped sailor shirt, known as "spirit of the sea" (海魂衫) paired with red scarf and a "national defense green" (国防绿) cloth bag.

During the Cultural Revolution, both the Young Pioneers and Youth League were disbanded as teens across China organized themselves into rival factions of Red Guards. Instantly identifiable by their red armbands, Red Guards leaving for their ideological instruction in Beijing had to prepare their own "uniform" of sorts, as described in Frank Dikötter's *The Cultural Revolution: A People's History*. This included a letter of introduction from the local Cultural Revolution committee, "a canvas shoulder bag, an aluminum flask, a tea cup, toothbrush and towel, and of course the ubiquitous Little Red Book, tucked away in a pocket or rolled in a quilt."

As reform and opening-up gathered steam in the 1980s, individual choices like wearing bright colors no longer brought accusations of "bourgeois tendencies," and Western fashions returned—indeed, government officials led the way by ditching their military costumes for a business suit and tie.

In 2001, logos for Beijing's application to host the 2008 Summer Olympic Games could be found on many primary students' uniforms

The modern-day Zhengzhou Experimental High School uniform has features designed and voted for by the student body

PHOTOGRAPHS BY FOTOE AND VCG

The tracksuit-style uniform so abhorred today first emerged in the 1990s, the culprit a 1993 notice from the Ministry of Education (then known as the China Education Committee) snappily titled "Suggestions Concerning Improving the Management of Urban Primary and Middle School Students' Uniforms."

The notice stipulated that uniforms ought to be "frugal, natural, lively, and functional," while stressing they are not the same thing as "exercise clothes" and that policies of a particular region ought to be made with support from "students, parents, and all levels of society." It also mentioned that designs should be based on the economic circumstances of the student body; the notice initially addressed only urban areas.

Officially associated with the Young Pioneers, the red scarf lingered on as a totem of loyalty; primary schools in the 90s often expected students wear them in a show of school pride.

Such expectations continue today, alongside varied other styles more in line with Western standards, such as slacks or pleated skirts. Increasingly, though, elite, independent, and boarding schools are adopting fashions that a student in the Republic of China might well recognize: long socks, collared shirts, sweater vests and ties. Meanwhile May Fourth suits are making a comeback on special occasions, such as graduation photos or assemblies commemorating the end of the war with Japan. Apparently, the school uniform, like history, has a way of repeating itself. - David Dawson, with contributions from Hatty Liu and Liu Jue (刘珏)

Originally published in May 2017

China Chic

Homegrown fashion from the drawing board to the shop floor

From utilitarian socialist garb to "sweatshop of the world" to insatiable appetite for luxury, China's tastes in fashion have seen stunning transformations in the last half-century. As the industry continues to mature, a new generation of domestic designers and brands are busy trying to find their voice and make homegrown styles competitive. We follow the making of Chinese apparel from the designer's imagination to the professional buyer's showroom, from the marketing offices of domestic brands to the eyes of fashion critics and consumers—and sees what's turning heads on the racks and runways.

Talking Shop

"The problem with most Chinese brands is that they just copy the looks of the West," remarks fashion enthusiast Emma Li, perusing racks of clothing at Beijing's APM Mall in Wangfujing.

"There are no design elements that make them inherently Chinese."

An HR manager by day, Li writes a style blog by night. "Why would I buy a Chinese brand, when it is just as economical to buy a foreign brand?"

Toeing the line between mainstream and traditional influences, however, is a difficult task. Leaning too heavily toward the mainstream, a brand can face accusations of simply copying Western designers. However, overly incorporating Chinese styles may limit the brand to the wallets of China's older generations—even as the government's policies promote homespun aesthetics.

"It is hard to be a designer here in China," notes Zhang Jing, who studied fashion design at the University of Arts in London before coming back to China and opening several high-end fashion stores in Beijing. "Most of the styles and colors are decided by European fashion houses."

"I think a lot of Chinese brands still copy from the West. Chinese designers need time to mature," believes Camila Li, an entrepreneur in her mid-30s who, with her penchant for designer purses and head-turning outfits, is typical of the country's newly affluent and fashion-conscious consumers.

Although a widely circulated February 2019 report by the Consumer Search Group claims that 45 percent of China's luxury buyers plan to purchase domestic designer brands within the next 12 months, Camila Li seems unlikely to replace her wardrobe anytime soon. "There are some brands, like Shanghai Tang, that utilize Chinese traditional elements like the *qipao*," she says, "But, I just don't see myself wearing those. Well, maybe once in a while."

Despite its name, Shanghai Tang is not even a fully homegrown brand; founded in 1994 by the late Hong Kong businessman David Tang, it was bought four years later by the Swiss-based Richemont Group. It returned to Chinese hands only some two decades later, when the Chinese private equity group, Lunar Capital, purchased it in December 2018.

The preference for foreign fashion has persisted despite moves by the government to curb its appeal. Foreign luxury brands were hit hard by the anti-corruption campaign, but now the market is being re-grown by the pocketbooks of middle-class consumers. Meanwhile, as Chinese manufacturers try to move up the value chain as part of the country's "Made in China 2025" plan, China Daily noted that "fashion designers in China are working to reinvent themselves as innovators."

No one embodies the drive for homegrown Chinese fashion brands more than China's "First Lady," Peng Liyuan. In 2013, the state media coined the hashtag #LiyuanStyle to praise President Xi Jinping's wife—famous in her own right as a folk singer—for using her public platform to promote Chinese designers, in particular Ma Ke of the brand Exception de Mixmind .

Overseas media quickly picked up on Peng's style, with Vanity Fair naming her the world's best dressed first lady; PopSugar listing her as one of their fashion icons; and Forbes hailing her for "inserting a dose of glamour into a traditional role."

While Weibo has nothing but praise for Peng's fashion choices, though, that buzz may not equate to sales for Chinese designers: No trendy label or fashion guru on Weibo has actually admitted to being inspired by Peng, while searching "Liyuan Style" doesn't turn up any results on online marketplace Taobao.

China's urban youngsters are yet to be convinced that

traditional Chinese elements represent the next wave of fashion, believing they reflect the tastes of the older generation. Meandering into Mandarin Collar, a sleek, minimalist store for men, Emma Li carefully examines the brand's dark blue and gray hues, coarsely spun cottons and linens, Chinese knots, and namesake collars. "I could never buy this and bring it home to my husband," she concludes, eyeing the 1,200 RMB price tag on one shirt. "This looks like something a man in his 50s or 60s should be wearing, not a man with a 3-year-old daughter."

At the clothing section of a state-owned commercial mall, filled with significantly older clientele, cashmere sweaters adorned with Sichuan opera masks, and a bright magenta *qipao* with a black faux-fur collar, equally fails to impress. "There is no way that these brands will survive in the upcoming decade," Li decrees. "Even my mother wouldn't wear these clothes."

Striking a balance between modern and traditional aesthetics may be the key for Chinese designers trying to differentiate themselves and remain relevant to China's fashion-forward urbanites—although it is easier said than done. "It is hard to take international fashion trends and put a Chinese spin on them," notes a male fashion editor in one of Beijing Central Business District's speakeasy bars.

Only a few are successful. "I love Shiatzy Chen," Li gushes, referring to the luxury fashion house founded by the so-called "Chanel of Taiwan," Wang Chen Tsai-Hsia. "[It] does a great job at taking traditional Chinese patterns and mixing them with Western-cut clothes."

Global trends don't pay much attention to tradition or geography. "The 2010s was all about streetwear in the fashion industry—and there isn't anything innately Chinese about that,"

Western and Chinese brands compete side-by-side in many shopping malls

Photographs by Vcg

Price-conscious shoppers will opt for domestic brands, often bought on Taobao says the editor. "But, you have a few brands like CLOT by [popstar] Edison Chen that are able to do it pretty well."

Despite the sex scandal that rocked his career a decade ago, Chen is serious about his new venture into fashion, calling CLOT "an initiative to bridge between East and West, China and America" in an interview with Forbes. A frequent collaborator with Nike, with stores on both sides of the Pacific, the label does not shy away from its "Made in China" connection. Far from it: CLOT's 2019 spring and summer promotional photos from Paris showcase t-shirts with cartoon images of dragons and cranes; hoodies with Chinese porcelain patterns; and even shirts with Chinese knot buttons.

"There are several Chinese brands getting a name in the West, but we shouldn't take it out of context," says Zhang, the designer. "A lot of people immediately start thinking about high-end brands. They forget that almost everyone in third, fourth, and fifth-tier cities are dressed exclusively in local brands." Indeed, in rural areas, the nearest clothing mall is often Alibaba's internet market place, Taobao, which allows cost-conscious, brand-ambivalent consumers to shop based on price point—a battle which local wholesalers will always win.

Cost is just one arena in which foreign brands have problems competing; fit is another. "Foreign brands aren't cut for the Chinese shape," complains Zhang, noting that most of her female customers opt for Italian business suits instead of unflattering dresses. "This means that Chinese brands are going to continue to survive."

Still, after over a decade in the Chinese market, foreign brands have begun to wise up. Visits to any mainland H&M or Gap will show that the stores offer predominately "petite fit" for women and "slim" for men, while some brands have gone to the next level, offering clothing specifically cut for the East Asian body shape (typically shallower front-to-back, and wider side-to-side). A plethora of brands have followed suit, such as Canadian athleisure bellwether Lululemon, which advertises its special "Asian cut" to China's next generation of yogis.

"When I visit the US, I sometimes have to shop in the children's section," laughs Emma Li. "Especially for shoes." While the average Chinese female shoe size is 5.5, most department stores in the US don't stock shoes smaller than 6. Normally, Li ends up buying items in the US that do not require a fit, like bags, scarves, jackets, jewelry, and sunglasses.

After a long day of window-shopping in Wangfujing, Li finally makes a purchase: An H&M leopard print t-shirt that was on sale for Chinese New Year. Before heading outdoors, though, Li bundles in up in a massive, eye-catching turquoise down coat, the kind that's ubiquitous across all regions and city-tiers of China. "Do you like it?" she asks. "As soon as I saw the color, I thought I had to have it. It was a good price too...I bought it on Taobao."

Designer China

It was the showstopper that launched a thousand memes, on both sides of the Pacific. But Rihanna's 2015 Met Gala dress, featuring a 55-pound gold cape by haute couture designer Guo Pei, was originally considered a risky move.

Organizer Anna Wintour had reportedly feared that the year's theme, "China: Through the Looking Glass," would end up seeming racist, or like a Chinese restaurant. Instead, bemused netizens PhotoShopped pizzas, omelets, and *jianbing* pancakes atop Rihanna's 16-foot yellow fox-fur trimmed train of

夾鏡鳴琴

資生德溥配坤元

茂育恩覃昭聖感

Cindy Wei Zhang often
seeks inspiration from
China's nature

Chinese floral embroidery, which took two years to make. The Washington Post, though, pronounced the evening "a thoughtful, expressive, and...utterly breathtaking exploration of China." And state media were quick to applaud, as China Daily claimed "Chinese elements help Met attendance reach record high."

Amid the triumphalism, there was frustration. While designers like Guo were enjoying the rare international exposure, Grace Chen, who has designed for both Oprah and Fan Bingbing, told Jing Daily that "the Western world has a huge misunderstanding of Chinese culture, and they don't even realize it."

Chinese media are usually quick to herald any major international event featuring homegrown designers as a watershed moment. "'Distinctly Chinese' elements stealing spotlight," crowed China Daily, again, after a "new wave of modern design that champions cultural elements from China" debuted at London Fashion Week in 2016, apparently delighting consumers "seeking Chinese-influenced design in their search for new identity and individual expression."

The reality is more nuanced. With a history dating back many millennia, as well as the aesthetics of 56 unique ethnic groups, "Chinese elements" are difficult to define. What does exist is an organic movement of young Chinese designers who are forging new markets by designing fashions that speak to their personal identity.

"When designers decide to make something 'Chinese,' some go for the most obvious thing: a *qipao*," points out 32-year-old Zhang Wei, who launched her eponymous brand, Cindy Wei Zhang, in 2012, after earning a degree in fashion from Australia's RMIT University. "Let's be honest, when is that last time you saw a woman wearing a *qipao* to go shopping? Never, right?"

"Chinese elements can be overpowering to a design," 33-year-old upstart designer Wang Mo opines. "Chinese designers can balance them because it is in our soul, but foreigners may have a difficult time." For example, when US first lady Melania Trump visited the Great Hall of the People in 2017, the black Gucci *qipao*-like dress that she wore, embroidered with pink phoenixes, was criticized by some for its "cheap" fur-cuffed pink sleeves.

There is little consensus about how to balance heritage with modernity, let alone proletarian aesthetics from the 1950s and 60s that are nostalgically making a comeback. Instead, designers often rely on their personal taste. "I cannot separate myself from my brand. I am Chinese, so naturally, my clothes have a Chinese feeling," says Wang, who came to her interview wearing unisex clothing from her own label -A (pronounced "minus A"), which champions neutral colors, sharp tailored lines, and fine fabrics. After nine years overseas, she viewed China's dearth of stylistic options as a call to action: "Clothes have a special power to them. When you wear high-quality clothes that match your personal style, you look completely transformed."

An enthusiast of traditional Chinese painting, Li Yalong moved to Tokyo to pursue his fashion studies, before returning to Beijing in 2017 and starting Yoikadakada. "I am made in China and I am proud of it," he declares.

Li is careful, though, not to add homegrown elements for the sake of it: "When Chinese aesthetics match my design concept, I definitely use them. But, I don't rely on any single one culture for my designs. I want everyone to be able to appreciate my collections, no matter what country they are from." (One of his most recent collections includes a purple jacket with big red Chinese characters saying " 堕落天使 ," Fallen Angel, on the back.)

Zhang, by contrast, actively seeks out local inspiration for her signature patterns. When starting a new collection, she visits historical sites and museums to photograph anything that she finds visually appealing, whether it's Tang dynasty lacquer or the guardian figurines on the roof of the Forbidden City. For the next month or two, she produces sketches based on her favorite images until she has perfected a pattern that can be replicated on her clothes.

In 2015, Zhang worked with her grandfather, a Traditional Chinese Medicine enthusiast, to create "Herbs," a collection which featured patterns of sinuous greens, bulbous pinks, and cellular blues. Each garment's inside tag described the medicinal effects of the plant that inspired it.

"I love to wear my own clothes; I love the patterns and the colors," Zhang says. Her designs were described by LA Fashion News as having "a purity of tone, exceptional handcrafting, and a quiet charm that has already resonated with peers."

Designers like Zhang say they are creating clothes they always wanted to wear, but never had the opportunity to before. Using fashion to express one's individuality is a relatively new concept in China. For decades after the founding of the PRC, clothes were made and patched at home with "cloth tickets" that rationed how much fabric someone could purchase.

Even after market reforms, "Chinese just had a few fashion brands to choose from, so their tastes were limited by the market options. People ended up buying the flashiest clothes they could find to show off their wealth"—a trend that persists to this day, according to Wang. "The more independent designers like me there are, the more the sophisticated Chinese tastes will become. It means that Chinese must start reflecting about who they are

EMERGENCY
EXIT

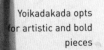

Yoikadakada opts
for artistic and bold
pieces

CAUTION CAUTION CAUTION CAUT

and what they think is beautiful," Wang believes. "Not only will this self-reflection benefit Chinese designers, but it will ultimately benefit Western brands, as well."

Buyer's Market

"The soul of a buyer shop is the taste of its buyer," says 31-year-old Xun Bing, a fashion buyer who now owns boutiques in Sydney and Shanghai.

Xun used to dream of being a designer, but after getting her bachelor's degree in the subject, she developed an interest in business, and looked for a way to combine it with her creativity. "It's not only about selling products, but presenting an attitude," she speaks of her current career, which involves trend-spotting and recommending promising brands and designers to shoppers who visit her stores.

In the fashion industry, buyers "are the link connecting brands, sales channels, and consumers," Hong Huang, fashion editor and founder of buyer store Brand New China, told Lifeweek magazine back in 2013.

Until recent years, though, buyers' role in the industry was probably the least well-understood—and not only by the public. "Through buyers and buyer shops, designers can learn more about the market," Hong explained. However, "lots of [independent] designers never have any contact with customers, but just open a little workshop for fun and stay in there tailoring and cutting all day...at most, a friend of theirs might say, 'I like your clothes, make one for me?'"

This amateurism wasn't just bad for designers; it hindered the spread of Chinese designs to the world. "[I've] been covering Chinese designers for eight years, but...when readers called to ask, 'I'm interested in that product you featured, where can I buy it?' I had to say, 'you can't,'" Hong told Lifeweek. "I realized I could devote pages to 'Designed in China,' but there was still a real distance before it can be brought to market."

Professional fashion buyers first appeared in Europe half a century ago, and today, most are still employed by international labels or department stores. Their main job is to attend trade shows, visit showrooms, and flip through lookbooks to source marketable styles and designers to sign.

It wasn't long, though, before some decided to strike out on their own, leading to the creation of multi-brand stores, or "buyer boutiques" (买 手 店) in Chinese. Operating like a niche-market personal shopping service, these stores curate some pieces for the showroom, but their real target customers are "professionals, mostly women...who don't want to appear at events in outfits that clash with anyone else's," and rely on buyers to scout out little-known brands, explained Hong. (Most are "second-generation rich" or overseas returnees, she added.)

Hong's Brand New China has cooperated with at least 150 Chinese designers, a far cry from when China's first buyer shop appeared in Shanghai in 1996. The buyer industry has taken time to develop in China. Luxury multi-brand store Galeries Lafayette's first flagship outlet closed only one year after its debut in Beijing in 1997. Lane Crawford's Shanghai store opened in 2000 and closed in 2006.

That all changed around 2010, thanks to China's growing middle class picking up the trend. According to a 2014 report by research firm RET and Fashion Trend Digest, four times as many buyer shops opened between 2010 and 2013 than the previous 14 years combined, with some even appearing in "second and third-tier cities."

By 2014 homegrown stores accounted for 55.6 percent of the mainland market for buyer stores. "[Middle-class] consumers have started to pursue individualistic and distinctive labels, with their interest gradually shifting from popular mainstream luxury brands to those that express unique personalities," opined Ye Qizheng, editor-in-chief of Fashion Trend Digest, to Jing Daily in 2014.

These buyers in turn created new platforms for local designers. In 2009, Beijing's Wudaoying Hutong saw the opening of Dong Liang, a multi-brand store featuring homegrown designs only. Since 2014, the store has hosted the "Dong Liang One Day" show at Shanghai Fashion Week every year, allowing Chinese designers to showcase their work. "We are like a window for the fashion industry from abroad to look at...Chinese creativity," boasted co-founder Tasha Liu to Time Out in 2011.

Xun believes that buyer stores like hers are on the cusp of a revolution. "Customers may be tired of the sales model in department stores." Online shopping, meanwhile, comes with no guarantees of quality or customer service.

But not everyone shares Xun's optimism. Chu Chu, a brand-employed buyer for Stuart Weizman, with nine years' experience in fashion industry, says that "successful buyer shops" are not as common as people think. They recently "boomed" simply because there were so few to begin with, and, as buyer Sun Ying told news site Jiemian in 2017, media hype had "misled people to think it's easy to run a buyer shop."

"Most buyer shops can only be seen in developed regions, which is far from enough to compete with e-commerce platforms," Chu adds. Taobao and other e-market places, in spite of their

Customers of most buyer boutiques are affluent

reputation for unreliable quality and copying, may be better—or at least less costly—bridges between independent designers and their market.

This means that, despite the odd successful shop that "discovered" and profited by launching the career of an unknown designer, most still bow to market pressure. "Maybe 10 percent of the goods [in the store] are there to show the buyer's class and taste, but make no profit, while the other 90 percent follow the market's trends," Chu estimates.

It's not all bad news, though. The fact that buyer shops are continuing to increase mean that "China's developing market has cultivated more mature customers and diversified aesthetic tastes," Chu believes. It only remains to be seen if their appetite can match that of China's buyers—or if the latter have bitten off more than they can chew.

Label Economics

"Our goats provide the very best cashmere in the world," claims Li Jing, CEO of 1436, the luxury fashion arm of one of China's best-known conglomerates, Erdos.

It's no empty boast: The company pays three times the price of their competitors for genuine *arbas* goat hair, which must meet exact standards—less than 14.5 micros in fineness and at least 36 millimeters in length, hence "1436."

The cost of these conditions is passed on to luxury buyers, Erdos's new target market, and the holy grail sought by every Chinese textile company seeking to establish their own brand. But while Erdos is held up as an exemplar of the state's "Made in China" industrial upgrade policy, it has the typical frustrations of a Chinese company balancing standards with cost—and a conflict between fierce capitalism and ecology on the Inner Mongolian plains.

Founded in 1980 in Ordos, a sparsely populated city in Inner Mongolia, Erdos originally capitalized on its access to the goats that produced some 70 percent of the world's raw cashmere supply. At the time, China was so poor that there was no machinery to process cashmere. "We had a special agreement with a Japanese company. They provided us with the machines and we exported our cashmere exclusively to them as payment for the first couple of years," explains Dai Tana, executive deputy general manager at Erdos.

As early as 1988, though, Chairman Wang Linxiang was already conceiving a cashmere brand for China's own affluent consumers, believing there were limits to the overseas business. This proved to be a tough sell: "It was necessary to educate consumers about what cashmere was, and why it was so much more expensive than wool," says Dai. Since most department stores were unwilling to buy cashmere, Wang left Erdos sweaters on consignment.

In the meantime, the export market remained a cornerstone of the company, which supplied cashmere to European fashion houses, such as Hermès, Burberry, and Loro Piana, as well as sweaters for American malls. "If you see a Lands' End sweater that says 'Made in China,' it's ours," an Erdos manager bragged to The New York Times in 1996. For that year's Christmas rush, Erdos had exported over 400,000 cashmere sweaters under Lands' End, Macy's, and J. Crew labels at a fraction of the cost of competitors in Europe.

With little competition, Erdos was quickly able to dominate Chinese market, but would struggle to maintain relevancy over the coming years. Once high-end foreign products flooded the market, Erdos was pigeonholed as "Grandpa's sweater" among younger consumers. To keep up, Erdos poached designers from international competitors, such as Hugo Boss and Giorgio Armani.

A more pressing problem was the effect of rampant capitalism on Erdos's backyard: Inner Mongolia was becoming increasingly deforested and barren, eroding the natural grazing habitat of the *arbas* goat. Since wool is sold by weight, opportunistic herdsmen began to crossbreed their *arbas* with other goat species with thicker and heavier hair, threatening the *arbas* with extinction.

Faced with this superfine cashmere crisis, Erdos took drastic measures, establishing an experimental herd of 8,500 *arbas* goats in the Otog Banner in Ordos, and creating the 1436 brand in 2006 to support the project. "Most of our customers have seen the world many times over," Li claims. "They can clearly feel the difference in the quality of our cashmere compared to others."

That said, 1436 products are still priced at one-half or two-thirds the price of foreign competitors, such as Loro Piana, though many of these companies still source their raw cashmere through Erdos. "Today, we have three main sources of revenue for our company," explains Dai: Erdos and 1436 for the domestic market; raw fiber exports; and supplying "finished cashmere products to foreign brands through long-standing partnerships."

Instead of providing their own model garments for Erdos to copy, some representatives of these foreign brands visit the Erdos showroom in Beijing to choose pre-made designs, which are later sewn with the foreign label. This practice is known in the industry as ODM (original design manufacturer), and, along with licensing agreements, is the key to how socialite Ivanka Trump or pop singer Jessica Simpson can create apparel brands without any background in fashion design.

"Many [Chinese] factories lack an understanding of sales and marketing," says Rachel Zheng, content curator for luxury news site Jing Daily. "So, they must rely on foreign partnerships with companies like Calvin Klein or UGG."

This means, though, that many "made in China" products could have been designed in China as well, even if they carry a foreign label. ODMs have also become "a timely topic—right now, [President] Xi Jinping is promoting the development and protection of intellectual property, as well as original innovations," says Zheng. "This means that many textile factories are actively transitioning to ODMs with their own design teams."

This is easier said than done, however. "Chinese people believe in the power of brands," says Zheng. "This is especially the case for high-end consumers...ODMs are popular among only value-

The *arbas* goat of Ordos provides superfine baby cashmere

conscious shoppers, especially in lower-tier cities." Some textile companies opt to acquire foreign brands: the Shandong Ruyi Textile Company purchased Bally for 700 million USD in 2018.

Erdos, as deputy general manager Dai stipulates, ensures that none of its foreign-labeled cashmere products are sold in the Chinese market, and recognizes the challenges of developing a sustainable brand. "So many of China's earliest fashion brands have already disappeared from the market," she notes. "We are constantly having to push ourselves to remain relevant."

For 1436 CEO Li, though, the mission is simpler. "In the past, 'Made in China' was often associated with things that are made cheaply or plagiarized. [Erdos] wants to show that 'Made in China' is something to take pride in." Or in other words: "Save a goat species; revive Chinese confidence in our national brands."
- Emily Conrad and Sun Jiahui (孙佳慧)

Originally published in March 2019

Kingdom of Lingerie

What the Chinese bra market reveals
about cultural trends

When Britpop band Suede—arguably the first major Western rock band to perform in China—played their legendary 2003 gig in the capital, a piece of lingerie was thrown onstage, according to Tian Yuan, who was the lead singer for Hopscotch (the now defunct band that supported Suede at the gig).

An unremarkable occurrence at many concerts, perhaps, but unheard of in China at the time and still incredibly rare today. Other witnesses report that the precise lingerie thrown may not have been your ordinary cup bra, but a *dudou* (肚兜), China's own unique answer to sexy undergarments—though it is difficult to prove the exact nature of the piece of 13 years later.

Chinese feminists may not have burned bras in defiance of the patriarchy as their 1960s American counterparts did, but China was a very different place at that time. It would, however, be a lazy generalization to imply that the role of Chinese lingerie has remained out of sight entirely in Chinese society, buried beneath layers of clothing and conservatism. The many sex shops that line the streets of Beijing tell a different story, and so too do the Chinese companies making massive profits from lingerie being sold not just in China, but also in the West and by stallholders in the developing world. While the market in China is set in certain ways, it is the exceptions that make it that much more interesting.

Revealing History

Despite its status as a homegrown item of lingerie, the *dudou*, or literally "belly cover," is a relatively rare garment in modern Chinese society, having long been jettisoned in favor of certain Western lingerie imports. It has, however, lived on as a form of backless top that sometimes contradicts the original designs by exposing the belly.

But evolution is in the very fabric of the garment, having changed multiple times over its very long history. A China Daily report put the origins of the *dudou* at the Qin dynasty (221 – 206 BCE), though arguably the report was using the interpretation that gave it the longest possible history, as multiple designs proliferated in the Ming dynasty (1368 – 1644), and it didn't really take its most well-known shape—a diamond piece of fabric with straps for the neck and back untill the Qing dynasty (1616 – 1911).

Chen Lihua, a Beijing-based clothing designer, told China Daily that "Young women often wore brightly-colored brocades of red, pink, or blue, as well as embroidered flowers, butterflies or mandarin ducks, which symbolize love, on the front of *dudou*." He also said that "Many ancient folk designs could be found on a dudou, including peonies, lotuses, cyprinoids, magpies and

Workers create padded lingerie at a factory in Guangdong province

mythical creatures. The themes were mainly about keeping good fortune and warding off disaster."

Zheng Zhenze, a professor at the Chinese Folklore Society, points out that the *dudou*'s modern evolution into something akin to a halter top would have been beyond the pale for those who had worn it in the conservative Qing dynasty, when it was strictly an underwear item. Wearing it in public would certainly have turned heads at the time, but would likely have brought about the unpleasant repercussion of being considered a "loose woman."

The *dudou* as a lingerie item still has its contemporary devotees. Although niche lingerie designer Irene Lu is not from China herself, when she encountered the *dudou* she developed an affection for it. "Personally, I think it's a beautiful cut," she told us, indicating that it makes a nice antidote to the "euro-centric" market in China.

Her lingerie company, Pillowbook, frequently uses the *dudou* as a central design in a deliberate move to differentiate itself from the heavily-padded, less comfortable alternatives that are commonplace throughout China. Indeed, it is the homogeneity of the lingerie market—with Chinese characteristics of course—that drove Lu to start her own company.

Uncomfortable Market

The lingerie market in China is fairly evenly divided between Chinese and Western-owned brands and is incredibly fragmented, with leading brands occupying 4 percent of the market at most, according to some frequently-cited estimates from market analysts. But these small pieces can still represent a massive amount of revenue—enough for one of the leading players, Aimer, to invest in a gargantuan factory with fancy architecture near the capital and set up research arrangements with a tertiary education facility.

In Guangdong province, which has long been China's manufacturing hub, the town of Gurao relies upon bra manufacturing. A Economist profile indicated that underwear made up 80 percent of its industrial output, including 350 million bras produced annually. As the economy slows down, times are looking grim for these underwear producers clustered around Guangdong, with many factories closing shop.

Citing market research company Frost and Sullivan, The Economist report stated that China makes 60 percent of the world's bras, producing 2.9 billion in 2014. That number would be roughly enough to provide every single adult woman in the world with a bra.

But it's important to differentiate between various sections of the market—the market trends in standard bras and comfortable underwear are distinct from those of racy lingerie. It is interesting to note that China's ongoing corruption crackdown hit many luxury products hard—expensive *baijiu* liquor saw massive declines, premium cigarette brands suffered, and so too did flashy car sales. But racy lingerie sales skyrocketed, likely in large part due to their very nature; while expensive liquor and cigarettes were bought to be passed around at banquets, and potentially seen by graft investigators, lingerie was only seen in the bedroom.

Thus, racy undergarments have been seeing solid sales. Aimer, for example, has been known to target well-heeled consumers in malls, using displays complete with customer support via an app, and activities like "guess your partner's bra size." These sizes are believed to have increased in recent decades, with most commentators attributing this to coming-of-age of women raised in a healthier economy.

But the sheer size of the market and its fragmentation does not necessarily lead to diversity in terms of form. "When I came to China, I was surprised to find that in such a huge market everything was so similar," Lu says, adding that she visits stores from time to time specifically to see if anything new has emerged, though it seems rare for that to occur. "Everything has padding," she points out. "I was tired of not being comfortable."

The Chinese lingerie market is geared toward heavily padded underwire bras to boost bust-lines. It's a common sentiment, as Chinese pop and sex culture are no less fixated on large breasts than their Western counterparts. "It can get fairly monotonous with all these heavily padded push-up bras," Lu says, "It's all about enhancing rather than embracing [the bust]."

In terms of style, colorful, exuberant bra designs are common, particularly in bright colors or patterns like leopard print, in contrast to Western customers looking for lacier designs. When Victoria's Secret entered the Chinese market with a local presence in 2015, it stuck strictly to the lower half of the lingerie equation as well as fragrances and beauty products, so it could conduct more research on customer preferences and ensure it didn't miss its mark and dissuade future customers. This comes as UK retailer Agent Provocateur launched its first store in Hong Kong, after already opening several in large mainland cities.

Evolving Garments

Lu points out that underwear has changed along with historical trends and that the US market has gone through periods where padded bras were heavily favored as well. "Think about the 1920s, when there was this emphasis on flattened chests, right through to women burning bras in the 1960s. There's always a link with how women perceive themselves.

"A lot of it comes down to feminism and women embracing their bodies...These are often highly educated women who are looking for something different."

She does admit with a laugh, however, that when she decided to launch a lingerie company that moves away from padded designs, "I was told it was impossible."

She turned her attention toward creating a very niche product—designs made to order from customer preferences, on a much smaller scale than the behemoths with massive factories around Guangdong, and increasingly, in countries in Southeast Asia with lower labor costs.

"Leftover women" (single women in their late 20s who are often

Chinese supermodel He Sui on the catwalk at the 2011 Victoria's Secret Fashion Show

put under pressure from meddling parents to get married) are a key market for more creative lingerie ventures, given their growing disposable incomes.

Turning Heads

The ways in which businesses explore the changing politics of lingerie, however, aren't always sophisticated. In November of 2015, a wily entrepreneur sought to distance himself from his rivals by creating a lingerie-themed bar, photos of which were circulated by the People's Daily Online. The bar was filled with various inflatable sex-dolls, all covered with lingerie, and bright pink and black ropes of bras covered the walls and ceilings. Most customers, however, appeared to come to have a drink, gawk at the scenery, and leave, so there seems to be little chance of it becoming a local cultural icon.

This business move, at least, was more tactful than a plastic surgery clinic which categorized parking spaces by bra cup size, generating more than a little mirth and outrage.

Not all recent projects have created an impression of half-baked get rich-rich-quick schemes, however. In a far more artful presentation, the People's Daily reported on the work of artist and jeweler Quan Qingsong in early 2016, who spent over three years creating a wearable bra sculpture made entirely of jade and gemstones.

The use of jade put a distinctively Chinese stamp on this piece of lingerie, though arguably, the most visible example of China's role in the global lingerie market comes, somewhat ironically, at dominant lingerie display of the US, the Victoria's Secret Fashion Show. It is now common practice to include Chinese fashion models such as He Sui and Liu Wen on the catwalk of the famous show, with the company no doubt eyeing the rapid growth and gains to be made in China.

And as the Chinese market grows and evolves, so too will its mark on global lingerie culture. - David Dawson

Originally published in May 2016

Vintage Vogue

As the market for thrift heats up, idealistic
vendors define what it means for China

Liu Ke's looks often allude to military themes. He owns US
Navy jackets, and it's not uncommon to see army insignia
sewn onto his pants. Today, doing light physical labor in
30-degree temperatures, he is "dressed down:" green fatigues, a
US Marines t-shirt, and leather shoes by a company that outfitted
naval officers during the Normandy landings.

These items are procured from cities like Seattle, Los Angeles,
and New York, which Liu visits around three times a year.
Aside from the clothes, these trips produce a bonanza of envy-
inducing photos for his social media feed. A jaunt in April to
Orange County boasted copious shots of blue skies and Elvis
memorabilia, earning a respectable 101 Weibo "likes."

But these posts aren't made just to show off: As owner of
Beijing's Mega Vintage, Liu is a leading member of China's
budding community of second-hand apparel clothing aficionados.

It's a role that requires converting wary consumers to a particular collectors' lifestyle, in addition to making sales.

Though it only opened in 2009, Mega Vintage is one of the oldest shops of its kind in China. Liu specializes in American apparel primarily from the 1920s to the 1980s, which qualifies as "vintage" in fashion circles (anything older is "antique"). "When I first started, there was a complete gap in the Chinese market," Liu says, "and what's more, unlike Western countries, we don't have this continuity in our fashion history: No cultural basis for appreciating, reviving, or improving old styles."

Elvis snapshots offer ways to partly fill this gap, educating followers about the culture his products come from, as well as allaying fears about thrift clothing, showing secondhand wear as commonplace. "In the US, vintage is very much part of how people outfit themselves every day, and these shops can be found anywhere, but Chinese people still have many prejudices about the concept," Liu says.

These stem mostly from a cultural aversion against buying secondhand—either the idea that it's a loss of face to wear another person's "castoffs," or superstition about used items containing the yin energy of previous owners—as well as persistent rumors that vintage clothing is actually "foreign trash" (洋垃圾). During the 1990s and early 2000s, factory rejects, donated castoffs, even clothes rumored to have been taken off dead people were regularly smuggled and sold in bulk in Chinese border towns; to many consumers who lived through that less-prosperous era, going vintage is no different.

Even more adventurous consumers among the urban middle class grapple with the fact that the origin, styles, and the historical eras of vintage items all tend to be foreign. This means there still isn't an exact Chinese translation for the concept of vintage. One can choose, like Liu, to scatter the English word in conversation like a trademark, or compromise, as other vendors and fashion bloggers do, along with the Chinese-sounding *guzhuo* (古着 , "old wearables")—which is actually a loanword from Japan. In the 1980s, Japanese consumers discovered *furugi* (as 古着 is read in Japanese) as a price-conscious way to keep up with global styles during an economic recession.

Today, in major fashion capitals of the West, charity and high-end consignment shops combine to offer a mix of preowned trash and treasure. But after authorities cracked down on the selling of "foreign trash" in the last decade, "vintage" or *guzhuo* in China now usually refers to high quality, one-of-a-kind items, curated from overseas at considerable time and expense by the vendors themselves—and as such, the industry is expensive, geared more toward fashion mavens and white-collar workers than broke students.

The prices reflect the market: Items rarely drop below the hundreds even in Liu's store, which claims to sell "everyday wear" from the era. For the handful of vendors specializing in luxury vintage, such as 80s Fendi luggage and 50s Chanel suits, items can run into the high thousands or tens of thousands—but are nonetheless snapped up by regular customers as soon as their photos appear on the vendor's social media account.

However, there are also businesses turning to Japanese *furugi* as a sometimes-cheaper alternative to Euro-American vintage. In lieu of a physical shop, vendors who are just starting out, have a day job, or live outside of major cities economize by starting an e-business, sometimes renting stalls with summer "vintage fairs," which tour the country and double as opportunities to hobnob with related interest groups, like indie jewelry-makers or vintage motorcycle fans.

Though welcoming of this diversity among his fellow vendors, Liu

PHOTOGRAPHS BY HATTY LIU, A-MAI AND VCG

1. Liu's Mega Vintage, opened in 2009 is considered the oldest vintage store in China

2. Silk blouses, often curated from Japan, feature at many Chinese vintage stores

3. Dressing the part is essential for many attendees at vintage fairs

4. Liu prefers to stock items steeped in American military and music history

5. Vintage Chinese garb is only starting to become popular in the market

is already afraid of an over-commercialized future. "Those who sell vintage simply because they think it's trendy, or do it for money, it's irresponsible," he insists. Liu even refuses to sell his wares online, unlike most of his colleagues, saying, "For this kind of product you need to come in and feel the ambience. Touch the clothes and try them on, talk to the owner, to feel its quality and understand its history, instead of just consuming a product or style."

These concerns still feel like remote luxuries for the growing body of merchants based in second and third-tier cities, though. Song Zihang, a shop-owner in Chengdu, admits he "almost never goes a day without explaining to a customer what vintage is." In Guangdong, formerly a hotbed for foreign goods hustled in via Hong Kong, vendor A-Mai says that her city is "always about half a step behind Beijing and Shanghai when it comes to fashion—we aren't very open-minded.

"We're still at the step of trying to get people to accept, then fall in love with vintage. My idea is that 'vintage' means it was 'loved' and cared for, not just used, by past generations," A-Mai says. "In that sense, to sell vintage is more like being a cultural ambassador than a merchant."

For Liu, on the other hand, this role is already filled by the clothes themselves. "They're objects for connecting with culture in the past," he says.

"When you see Doc Martens being revived in the streets, traces of military 'Ringer tees' on items at Zara or Uniqlo, instead of just buying it because you think it looks nice, you can find out how these styles were inspired and how people used to wear them," he adds. "That's the experience I want to provide." - Hatty Liu

Originally published in September 2017

PHOTOGRAPH BY A-MAI

Fashion-forward vendors like A-Mai struggle to find acceptance for their style in smaller cities

Chapter Two:
Food

"People regard food as Heaven."

- Chinese idiom

The Anatomy of Cake

How a culinary import responds to local culture

Despite centries of debate, the culinary community has still reached no consensus on the affinition of cakes. Simply put, a cake can be any type of bread conditioned by extra air bubbles and one's own cultural expectations for how desserts ought to taste.

In the case of the nine-inch layer cakes now ubiquitous in bakery shop windows across Chinese cities, this is a perfect recipe for crossed cultural wires and disappointment.

Consider the appearance of the typical American bakery cake— an airy foundation of an oven-baked, eggy concoction, coated with a layer of what those in the English-speaking world call "frosting" or "icing." Yet the words "frosting" and "icing" definitely recall a texture of crystallized sugar and crunchy glaze that the Chinese bakery cake shares neither in composition nor taste. Instead, the Chinese bakery cake is glazed by *naiyou* (奶油 , "milk oil"): a fluffy mass of cream, or more commonly, vegetable oil-based whipped topping, only lightly tinged by a sweet taste. They often come topped with fresh fruits, and the creamy glaze can dry up or break down after an hour or so left in the open air. Underneath, the base is typically a sponge cake held up by beaten egg whites and filled with more cream and fruit.

Next to similarly tiered-and-glazed Western staples like the German chocolate cake, Boston cream pie, or the basic buttercream sheet cake, it's no wonder the strangeness of Chinese cake and dessert is a perennial topic of expat blogs. Meanwhile, online baking and decorating communities see routine recipe requests from overseas Chinese consumers and cake decorators that clarify it is the elusive cake of their childhoods that they want, not that diabetes-inducing American stuff.

On the flip side, hordes of Chinese diners who encounter sugar-based frosting or icing, pound cake, custard, and chocolate-cream filling have had a one-word response to these Western culinary staples: *ni* (膩), a difficult-to-translate word that describes a nauseating feeling from over-exposure to a single taste. In the case of "Western desserts," they usually mean that the taste is too sweet, though sometimes they also mean it's too oily or rich. Whether your preferred poison is marzipan or meringue, fondant, or the typical American buttercream, *naiyou* remains several magnitudes lighter and blander than all of these; the tartness of the fruit also breaks up the monotony of grease and sugar.

A Chinese fan of TLC's *Cake Boss*, who took it upon herself to personally go sample Buddy Valastro's creations in New York, made up this memorable summary of the experience in a web forum: "Ate some, wasn't good; everything was overly sweet, but foreigners like it pretty well."

Cream and fruit-based desserts make up the majority of China's cake aisles

Stereotyped as a nation of rice-eaters, it can be easy to forget that wheat-based foods and desserts have their own indigenous roots in China. In ancient times, the overland and maritime Silk Roads did brisk trade across Asia in desserts such as baklava and ingredients like nuts, dried fruits, almond paste, and eventually sugar cane and vanilla. However, globally, the concept of "cake," as a flour-based concoction made with refined sugar and raised by beaten eggs (rather than unleavened or raised by yeast) was associated with Europe toward the mid-seventeenth century, doubtlessly helped by the large-scale cultivation of sugar cane in the New World colonies. This history is reflected in the names of the culinary certificates at places like the Beijing New East Cuisine School; mastering wheat-flour creations like *bing* (饼) makes you an expert at "Chinese-style flour-based snacks (中式面点)," but knowledge about making and decorating cake (蛋糕) falls under the curriculum of "Western-style flour-based snacks" (西式面点), or simply "Western snacks" (西点).

The earliest and clearest genealogy of a European-influenced style of sponge cake becoming an East Asian dessert tradition belongs to the Japanese *castella*. Brought to Japan by Portuguese merchants in the 16 century, this is a honey-flavored cake raised by egg whites without the aid of butter or other oil.

It is less clear when the European-influenced cake made landfall in China. According to the court writings of the Qing dynasty, the Qianlong Emperor and Emperess Dowager Cixi were both reportedly fond of a snack called *caozigao* (槽子糕), a small round cake specially baked for breakfasts in the imperial court out of fresh eggs, white sugar, and flour. The character *cao* (槽, mould) referred to the instrument for baking the cake, and was used because *dan* (蛋, egg) was inauspiciously associated with curses and insults in the imperial capital. It is now considered a local delicacy in Beijing and Tianjin.

References to Western-style restaurants in Chinese cities and European-inspired desserts being consumed by the elite classes in the imperial capital can also be found in the Qing dynasty writings such as the *Record of the Awakened Garden* (《醒园录》), which contains a section of recipes on preparing the most fashionable desserts and confections of the mid-eighteenth century. Qing dynasty records tell us that by at least the nineteenth century, Western desserts had become commonplace enough in China to be grouped into five categories: meringues, "wet" desserts (such as ice cream), bread, crispy pastries such as cookies, and cake. The cake is said to be a type of "cream cake" that tastes "soft and spongy."

In terms of taste, texture, and the method of preparation, cakes in China appeared to have already developed a style of their own by the eighteenth century. In the *Record of the Awakened Garden*, compiled in 1782, the primary mode of cooking both egg-based

The Chinese *bing* is a traditional flour-based snack

dangao (蛋糕) and "Western cake" was by steaming. This would have provided a softer, airier, and moist texture to an otherwise familiar set of steps to a modern-day baker, calling for a ratio of a pound of flour, 10 eggs, and a half-pound of white sugar evenly mixed and set to rise, then steamed until "chopsticks can be inserted without sticking" and served once it is "cooled and cut in slices." Those making the "egg-based cake" also have the option of making a "dry cake" by warming up the mixture on a stove before baking in a small metal furnace. The "Western cake" in the eighteenth-century China called for 16 eggs for every pound of flour and half pound of white sugar, as well as half a bowl of sweet rice wine and water. After "mixing by using chopsticks" and "blowing away the foam," the batter must be left somewhere warm to rise, and then wrapped securely in cloth before being placed in a bamboo steamer.

The commercial bakery offering Western-inspired birthday cakes, danishes, shortbreads, and other pastries had their start in the 1980s and 90s on the Chinese mainland, helped by market reform as well as the techniques and adaptations for taste developed by bakeries in Hong Kong. Well-known Chinese bakery chains such as Holiland and Christine were both founded in 1992, later joined by chains such as Weidome, Auspicious Phoenix, Ichido, and Kengee. It was also around this time that it became tradition in China to serve cake at birthday celebrations, which were and still are partly associated with foods such as noodles, symbolizing longevity, and boiled egg, symbolizing "rollover onto the next year."

Today, however, the fruit-and-*naiyou* bakery cake is more or less referred to by default with the term "birthday cake," while more elaborate, artistic, fondant-based cakes for weddings and expositions tend to be the job of boutique bakeries and specialty chains such as Black Swan rather than the commercial bakery. If the search results of group-buying sites are any indication, in more recent years mousse cakes featuring stencilled-on astrological signs are becoming the trendy option in birthday cakes. The absence of ovens in most Chinese homes makes DIY cake-decorating sessions a popular offering at commercial bakeries as a birthday treat for one's children and friends.

The icing vs. *naiyou* distinction aside, another point of departure between the English and Chinese language of cakes is that a cake in Chinese is not a cake until it is properly garbed. The early example from the Qing records aside, the modern word *dangao* refers usually to the final product on the shelf once it is coated in *naiyou* and decorated, while the part that comes out of the oven is more accurately the base, not to be sold or consumed separately.

The difference in the texture of *naiyou* and sugar-based icing leads to several unique cake-decorating techniques and patterns found among Chinese bakeries. Although cream is less stable and breaks down more quickly than sugar-based icing, a skilled decorator will be able to pipe the same types of decoration with the same level of intricacy. However, the lines, borders, and the edges of flower petals made with *naiyou* are noticeably smoother and shinier, with a rounded and flowing appearance compared to the jagged and stiff textures of icing or fondant. The fruit or chocolate garnishes can also be cut and arranged into creative patterns to give a vertical dimension to the cake.

The 12 animals of the Chinese zodiac, the red-tipped "longevity peach," *mah-jong* pieces, and the bearded "old sage of longevity," are staple Chinese decoration on birthday cakes. These can be piped directly onto the cake using cream as three-dimensional figures, which, according to the evaluation forms for job applicants at the popular chain bakery Auspicious Phoenix, is a required skill for their decorators. To make a bearded sage, which is a common motif used in birthday cakes for the elderly, the decorator puts a wide-tipped piping bag close to the surface of a cake and slowly builds the feet, body and eventually the head by squeezing in a circular motion, then smoothing the figure and adding details with a small brush. The hair and beard are then piped onto the body with a small parchment bag, with the silky texture of the *naiyou* giving complement to the mystical, flowing hair and robes of the old immortal. Alternatively, the cake base might be cut into small pieces that are then used to make the base of a three-dimensional figure, or else the figure might be pre-made out of chocolate.

Due perhaps to the sensitivity of *naiyou* to room temperature and heat from the decorator's hands, typical cream-based Chinese bakery cake decorations are meant to be completed in a short amount of time. Provided you don't visit at a busy time or with an abnormally complicated order, you can walk into most bakeries in China and leave with your decorated birthday cake in 30 minutes or less. Online tutorials for making three-dimensional cake decorations usually clock in at five to ten minutes even including explanations. There is also a sub-genre of videos, aimed at professional and amateur decorators, where the primary appeal seems to be watching the decorator pipe the most complicated figure in as short a time as possible, usually one to two minutes. *Cake Boss* has got some competition. - Hatty Liu

Originally published in July 2016

Quick Fix

Can China save its struggling fast food industry?

Mr. Lee, the fast-food chain formerly known as "California Beef Noodle King," is a source of annual bemusement for my overseas relatives on their visits home. "What do beef noodles have to do with California?" my father or uncle ask, without fail, each time they encounter the restaurant's signs in a Chinese train station and airport lounge.

The answer—quite a lot. Mr. Lee, which calls itself China's oldest domestic fast-food brand, has its roots in a Los Angeles beef noodle restaurant founded in 1972 by P. C. Lee, a Chinese-American businessman born in Chongqing. Corporate lore claims that an unnamed "major American fast food chain" approached Lee in the 1980s, when he already had a small empire of seven shops with top reviews in the Los Angeles Times, and asked him to be its partner in China, the emerging market already being eyed by industry juggernauts like McDonalds and KFC.

But instead of taking this offer, Mr. Lee decided to move his entire business, head office and all, to China. According to one customer's reminisces on Weibo, the 1988 opening of the first "California Beef Noodle King USA" in Beijing drew lines comparable to the city's first KFC, which launched the year before. Despite its unremarkable food, already available at hundreds of thousands of mom-and-pop noodle shops and ordinary homes, the restaurant seduced diners with its sleek interior and Western cachet—the name, the machine-like efficiency of its preparation system, and its claim to be the first Chinese restaurant in the country to offer canned soft drinks.

Today, though, the noodle king—since renamed "Mr. Lee" in memory of its founder, who passed away in 2008—is firmly classified among domestic Chinese brands, whose inability to achieve international recognition on a par with foreign chains like Panda Express and Taco Bell is bemoaned regularly by industry experts. Having opened around 800 locations, after 30 years in the business, Mr. Lee is the most prolific of the national chains. The next biggest is Zhen Gong Fu, "Real Kun¬g Fu," founded in Guangdong province in 1997, with 600 shops.

By comparison, there are over 5,000 KFC locations on the mainland alone, making it China's biggest restaurant chain. McDonalds follows, with 2,500 locations, even though it arrived in China two years *after* Mr. Lee. For further contrast, the American burger franchise had over 1,000 restaurants in its home country by 1968, after just 13 years in business; by 1978, McDonalds surpassed 5,000 outlets and has barely stopped growing.

Restaurant owners are wondering where Chinese chains went wrong. In 2014, a much-publicized food scandal, in which a Shanghai supplier was found to be repacking expired meat for

PHOTOGRAPH BY VCG

Chinese fast-food dishes are typically combo meals with rice

several US fast food chains, was tipped as a possible turning point in the fortunes of domestic chains. Those hopes, though, have since petered out—if anything, Chinese brands seem even less competitive than before. According to a 2017 study by Caiyinren Bidu, a social media account for the fast food industry, brands like Real Kung Fu and Yonghe King have seen their growth plateau since at least 2013, while the listed value of Real Kung Fu fell by 50 percent from 2012 to 2015 due to internal scandals.

"Are Chinese 'lower-end' restaurant [chains] under a curse?" asked one 2016 study by Shenzhen consulting firm Gelonghui. Real Kung Fu co-founder Pan Yuhai has called the present state of the industry a "bottleneck," while Yi Zhengwei, restaurant consultant and co-founder of the chain restaurant 72Street, more specifically called it "a curse...to do with standards." In a 2015 essay, Yi writes, "if you just want to invest in a Chinese fast food restaurant, you can easily become a leader in the [domestic] market. But if you actually want to be great, you can think again."

In *The Founder*, the 2016 biopic of McDonalds co-founder Ray Kroc, an iconic moment is when anti-hero salesman Kroc pulls up at the McDonald brothers' diner in the desert, and finds his food ready just seconds after ordering. More central to the story, though, is what comes afterwards, when one of the brothers shows a slack-jawed Kroc the well-coordinated dance that leads to their speedy and identical delivery: "Every McDonald's burger has two pickles, a pinch of onions, and a precise shot of ketchup and mustard."

Yi believes that, in China, the speed and ingenuity of food prep are not the chief struggles of its "fast" food industry. After all, it's a nation where stores have whole aisles devoted to vacuum-packed instant meals, where roadside vendors can cook and roll up a *jianbing* with egg and *baocui* in a minute flat. The reasons China struggles, as Kroc would say, to "franchise the damn thing from sea to shining sea," seem to lie in three areas: standardization, quality, and branding.

As with every modern Chinese practice, there have been recent attempts to find indigenous roots for fast food in ancient literature. In this case, it's a type of eighth-century banquet know as the *liban* (立办): According to the *Tang Dynastic History Supplement* (《唐国史补》), a courtier named Wu Cou received a major promotion from the emperor, but had little time to celebrate before he had to report to work. His solution: order every course brought to the table before his guests arrived (the idea apparently caught on).

The modern *kuaican* (快餐)—literally, "fast meal"—actually predates the arrival of Western chains in the late 80s and 90s, and refers to a type of no-frills diner or roadside stall, popular with blue collar

A Shenyang Real Kung Fu branch combines Chinese aesthetics with familiar accoutrements of a fast food chain

workers. Still common in "third-tier" or smaller cities, *kuaican* vendors offer cut-rate combo meals with rice and entrees kept in steam trays similar to overseas Chinese buffets, or roadside "one dollar Chinese food" joints in the US, in all but the actual food.

KFC adopted the term when it landed in Beijing in 1987, calling itself *meishi kuaican* ("American-style fast food"), and changing the connotation of a quick fix forever. When KFC published the recollections of its original restaurant's employees in 2017, they unanimously agreed the speed and (rather greasy) Western food were not what impressed Chinese diners 30 years ago. Rather, the uniformed cashiers (hired with strict height requirements), "white-gloved" sanitation staff, and "95 percent imported equipment," down to the cutlery and pictures on the wall, all spoke of modernity and modishness to 80s Chinese society. "If it happened today, people would post pictures of it every day on

WeChat Moments," claimed employee Sun Zhijun.

As fast food fever began in the 90s, the government tried to push for an official definition of *kuaican*. In 1997, the Ministry of Domestic Trade published guidelines that determined it as "cuisine for the masses that satisfies the demands of the consumer's everyday life," and "fast to prepare, convenient to eat, standardized in quality, balanced in nutrition, handy of service, and economical in price." The same year, the ministry named Beijing's Quanjude Roast Duck, Tianjin's Goubuli Baozi, and Shanghai's Ronghua Chicken (a KFC competitor, later replaced with Lanzhou *lamian*) as the "Big Three" of Chinese-style fast food.

Helped by these influential "time-honored brands," the ministry hoped to see domestic *kuaican* take 30 percent of the market by 2010, fulfilling Premier Li Peng's directive of "fast food with national characteristics [and] scientific-scale management." It didn't work. Aside obvious differences in aesthetics, cooking methods, and management styles compared to Western upstarts, Yi points out that "time-honored" foods, by definition, market themselves on local history, memories, and taste—the antithesis of a brand trying to go global.

"American food culture is generally unified—hamburgers, pizza—so McDonalds can open tens of thousands of stores, whereas Chinese *kuaican* are examples of what's most authentic, grassroots, and popular in a region," he writes. "The South likes rice, the North likes noodles; the East likes sweet, and the West likes savory."

There's also little standardization among Chinese brands. According to Gu Zhenyu, author of a 2002 study on the growth of *kuaican*, Chinese cuisine has historically relied on the skill and reputation of individual chefs, with personal recipes and local tastes being the arbiters of excellence. An additional problem is that restaurants are unwilling to spend money on employee training, and even the biggest brands still rely on traditional "manual preparation" over more consistent machines and assembly lines. "It's already well known that Chinese-style *kuaican* has inconsistent quality," Gu's report noted, suggesting that this also leads to "perception of lack of care toward sanitation and nutrition."

"When a [Chinese *kuaican*] product tries to 'go out into the world,'" Yi concludes, "it meets with pain everywhere."

The government's decision to push time-honored brands hasn't stopped new *kuaican* upstarts from trying to adapt the Western models and please every regional palate. Mr. Lee's chief rival, Real Kung Fu, started under another name in 1990. By 1997, it was promoting a so-called "computer programmed steaming process" for its rice dishes and entrees, which promised to deliver from kitchen to counter in 80 seconds or less.

Real Kung Fu refused our request for details on their process— "these are our trade secrets," said the manager of one location— but periodic "Open Kitchen Days," typically held at different locations nationwide on March 15, China's Consumer Protection Day, reveal that the food is simply pre-prepared and packaged in individual servings at a central kitchen prior to delivery. With each order, kitchen staff simply pops the item into its designated "steam cabinet" programmed with a temperature and timer. The forced steam reheats the item in record time, and the meal is then taken out and assembled on the tray.

This "digitalization" extends to clean-up, as one location

manager proclaimed to journalists at a media session: "All cutlery is soaked for at least three minutes; rubber cutlery at 40 to 50 degrees Celsius, stainless steel at 50 to 60 degrees." A repertoire of "hash-house" lingo is also crucial for the appearance of efficiency and success; Real Kung Fu servers have the habit of shouting *dabai* (大白, "big white") for every bowl of rice the customer orders. At Dr. Tian, a bargain-basement competitor in the steamed-rice-combo trade, the cashiers' cry of a dish's primary characteristic—"spicy!"—"meat!"— is taken up by the kitchen staff, in a sort of supply chain call-and-response, before the meal is served with *xiaobai* (小白, "small white"), their slang for rice.

Mr. Lee, though, may have perfected standardization. "I can't talk about our process," says location manager Su Li—seemingly the standard response—but, "It's because I can't explain it. Everything just arrives the way it is, and we are just the 'front line' staff. When the customer orders, we're responsible for serving it. It's that simple." Behind her, a TV screen loops a video of Mr. Lee's entrepreneurial story, ending with footage of a factory in suburban Beijing where "beef is sliced into two centimeter-wide cubes" and mixed in large vats with "broth from 18-month-old hens" and uniformly cut noodles. "Modern, nutritious, the taste of quality," the narrator intones.

For some customers, however, the near-complete mechanization of *kuaican* is a step too far. On Q&A platform Zhihu, the question "Why is Chinese-style *kuaican* universally said to be expensive and terrible-tasting?" has been viewed over 15,000 times. One users claims that "mechanization leads necessarily to bad flavor, compared to the handmade," whether it's Western or Chinese *kuaican*; however, Western brands have better ads and "psychological influence" on the consumer. Similar threads on

Many Chinese restaurants struggle to combine traditional cooking methods with rapid kitchen-to-counter delivery styles

Baidu, Guokr, and Douban had users chiming in, "every Chinese chain tastes the same" and "you can't even call [the dishes] real Chinese cooking."

What would make a Chinese diner go for *kuaican* in a nation full of independent eateries with even cheaper prices, longer hours, and better (or at least more varied) fare? For now, it appears that Chinese fast food joints mostly compete on perceptions of sanitation, and location, however precarious these could be. Chain restaurants, Yi notes, have the resources to open in malls and commercial arteries, while small businesses converge around residential areas; illegally converted storefronts, meanwhile, are at the mercy of officials and developers.

"I'm surrounded by small restaurants where I live...rice noodles, beef ball noodles, Hakka noodles, congee stands...but I'm afraid to eat there too often, due to all the additives," says Li Han, an occasional fast food diner from Guangzhou. As one Guokr commenter puts it, even bland *kuaican* is "better than gutter oil."

Yet in both quality and location, writes Yi, Chinese *kuaican* is beaten by Western chains with even deeper pockets and a brand loyalty developed over decades. In any commercial area of a first-tier city today, one can easily find a Mr. Lee's, KFC, Real Kung Fu, and McDonalds clustered together, sharing the same chrome-topped tables that had awed first-time *kuaican* customers over 30 years, their walls all covered with faddish faux-chalk writing. The Chinese chains also have their own mascots—the eponymous Mr. Lee, and a yellow-clad martial artist that Real Kung Fu (dubiously) insists is not modeled on Bruce Lee.

When we visit one such Beijing strip at 3 p.m., the lull between lunch and dinner, the Chinese locations were all but empty, while their Western neighbors were still standing-room only. Children were noticeably absent from the domestic outlets, while in McDonalds, they were screaming enthusiastically for their next Happy Meal (with dessert and tie-in merchandise).

Li says her daughter "will ask to eat [at McDonalds], but doesn't really know any Chinese *kuaican* brands." Instead, when the 12-year-old wants Chinese food, "I can just make it at home, since I'm a housewife." Another mother of an 11-year-old at KFC, surnamed Yu, agrees. "My son will actively ask to eat Western food; he likes fries, chicken nuggets, and ice cream. I'll take him to KFC or McDonalds if his grades have been good or if it's a holiday."

These near-cultish associations of fast food with novelty and childhood ritual, cultivated by Western brands over several decades, are completely out of reach of Chinese firms. In the wake of the 2014 food scandal, some media looked to Real Kung

Jianbing is one rapidly cooked Chinese snack that's seeing international franchising

Fu as a contender for a domestic fast food revolution: It had the most recognizable (if arguably copyright-infringing) logo and made a minimum effort at community outreach, hosting Open Kitchen Days and hiring Bruce Lee lookalikes to put on kung fu shows.

Yet within a year, the company's listed value had tumbled to an all-time low as the private scandals of the company's two founders—who both served as CEO, and were also ex-brothers-in-law—began to leak out. In 2006, co-founder Chen Dabiao secretly divorced his wife, whose brother Pan Yuhai had been Chen's original business partner. In the ensuing struggle over control of the business, Chen had been ahead, until news of his affair spread in 2009—and in 2011, it emerged he had been deceiving not only his wife, but investors and shareholders, moving capital and siphoning funds. Chen was sentenced to 14 years in prison, but the chain's value, to say nothing of its reputation, has never recovered.

Today, business journals cite the saga as a cautionary tale for the family-owned enterprise, a model that describes an estimated 90 percent of restaurant businesses in China big and small. Yi, though, remains optimistic about the future of *kuaican* in China, pointing out that it was only in 2008 that the GDP in Guangzhou, where his 72Street restaurant chain was headquartered, had surpassed the US GDP circa 1955, the year after which McDonalds began its expansion.

"The time is yet to come for *kuaican* to become a part of everyday life," he declared. Diner Yu is more skeptical. "We go to [Chinese chains] too; [but] their taste just still hasn't caught up," she says. And not just the taste, but the amenities—on a sweltering afternoon in mid-June in Beijing, KFC was the only restaurant on the street with air-conditioned temperatures below 25 degrees. - Hatty Liu

Originally published in July 2018

Veggie Values

Spurred by health concerns and Buddhist
benefits, vegetarianism is taking root in China

Xing Lihong decided to go vegan after spending a week at the
Donglin Temple, Jiangxi province, in the summer of 2005.
But she'd been readying herself for the decision since 2002, when,
after reading Buddhist and nutritional texts, she began abstaining
from meat on the first and fifteenth of every lunar month.

"At first, I felt hungry and craved for meat," Xing confessed.
"I often ate a lot after the two 'vegetarian days,' as a form of
compensation." But gradually she got used to the new regimen.
"I'm convinced that 'everything has a spirit,' and it's this belief
that makes me stick to it."

Xing is just one of a growing number of Chinese choosing to
reject a traditional carnivorous diet in favor of a meat-free life.
There are now around 50 million vegetarians in China, Xinhua
estimates—about 3.5 percent of the population.

"In the future, China will become the number one vegetarian

country," predicts Tang Li, founder and head of the Chinese Vegetarian Association. "It's just a matter of time." The association, a non-profit that promotes the benefits of a vegetarian diet, was established in 2007, and is made up of ordinary vegetarians, entrepreneurs, activists, and nutritionists.

A vegan himself for 25 years—a philosophy that abjures all animal products, from meat and dairy to leather and gelatin— Tang believes the increasing popularity of vegetarianism is partly because the "government has become more and more open-minded to Buddhism." According to the non-partisan Pew Research Center, there are approximately 245 million Buddhists in China—around 18 percent of the total population. Another 21 percent adhere to folk religions that incorporate Buddhist beliefs.

Tang offers four main reasons for the diet's growth: "The first is health, as some people are forbidden from eating meat by their doctors; second is wealth, as many become vegetarian because they stepped into the vegetarian industry.

"The third is out of curiosity, as some people just imitate vegetarian celebrities; lastly, belief—Buddhism is pretty popular in China, and its non-pacifist doctrine is leading China to become a big vegetarian country."

In Xing's case, religion and health were her main considerations. A vegan for 13 years, Xing is now more adamant than ever that her decision was right—and even thinks it helped ward off bad luck. "It's really magical," she tells us. "I have always been hardworking and capable, but in the past things happened for no reason—my first workplace shut down, then my second workplace fired me, though they later told me that was a mistake. I didn't know what was wrong, so I guess my only misdeed was eating animals."

A Shandong traditional culture center offers a free vegetarian lunch of four dishes and a soup to locals; the center promotes the spirit of "great love" by opposing the killing of animals

"Unbelievably," says Xing, "after I quit meat, my luck came back. Everything's going very well now."

Regardless of her claims to karma, Xing can point to her improved health as a tangible benefit. "I had been weak and sickly since I was a child," she says. Things were no better in her first two years of veganism, when she often seemed pale and weak. But now, aged 49, Xing is in peak condition: "I have only had two colds in the past 13 years," she claims.

In fact, Xing says her family has a tradition of vegetarianism: Her great-great-grandfather and great-grandfather were both apparently vegans from childhood, while her grandmother and two of her great-aunts barely touched meat their whole lives. All were blessed with longevity, with her female forebears living up to 97, 98, and 99 years (her great-grandfather perished early, at 73, due to famine in 1963).

"None of them ever stayed in bed or needed medicine, nor did they have any chronic disease," boasts Xing, who is convinced that the secret lay with their diet. "They could all look after themselves in their late years. Based on this, I really believe that 'Diseases find their way in from the mouth,' and a meat-free diet does have a decisive influence on health."

Dr. Xiao Changjiang, Head of the Cardiovascular Department at the Hunan Academy of Traditional Chinese Medicine (TCM) Affiliated Hospital, believes that a vegetarian diet is more suited to the Han Chinese than a carnivorous one. "As a farming people, the Chinese had adopted a plant-based diet since ancient times," Dr. Xiao says. "We are less tolerant to meat than nomadic people. Since the 1980s, the massive supply of meat resulted in people eating much more of it."

"The past three decades have seen a striking increase in the prevalence of chronic non-communicable diseases, like coronary heart disease and diabetes." says Dr. Xiao, "It's related to the surging consumption of meat."

For decades since the PRC's founding in 1949, eating meat was a luxury for most families, and usually reserved for special occasions such as weddings or festivals. But as the country grew wealthier since the 1980s, meat on the table became a sign of increased prosperity. In 2007, the United States Department of Agriculture estimated that China consumed about 74 million tons of pork, beef, and poultry that year, considerably more than any other country, and around twice as much as the US.

The same year, according to the World Health Organization, China laid claim to having both the most diabetes patients—10 percent of the adult population, compared with less than one percent in 1980—and the highest number of mortalities from the disease in the world. A 2016 study, published in British medical journal The Lancet, noted that about two-thirds of Chinese aged 40 to 59 were overweight or obese.

In April 2017, Dr. Xiao, in cooperation with the non-profit organization Daohexiang, launched the Vegetarian Ward at the Hunan Academy of TCM Hospital in Changsha. The project promoted a "One Vegetarian Meal Per Week" plan by providing free vegetarian dishes to both patients and hospital staff. "It's an experience-based activity," Xiao explains. "We invite the patients to try the meal and then explain the benefits to them. This will make it easier for them to accept." The scheme has so far served more than 7,000 people, and the feedback has been "pretty good."

Yet there are concerns, and pushback from some quarters. On popular Q&A site Zhihu, the question "What are the side effects of having a vegetarian diet?" has attracted more than 200 answers.

"Doesn't it cause malnutrition?" many wondered.

"If one doesn't eat vegetables properly, it may cause malnutrition. But being vegetarian itself is completely fine," Dr. Xiao confirms. The key is a balanced diet that's "as varied as possible," which means consuming all types and parts of plants—from roots, leaves, flowers to seeds, fruits, starches, and stems.

In the vegetarian ward, "We don't force people to become vegan directly, because it's not easy and often requires people to have some nutritional knowledge," says Dr. Xiao. "We are just suggesting, especially to those suffering from cardio or cerebrovascular disease, that they should increase the proportion of plants in their diet." In April 2018, the Changsha Hospital of Integrated TCM and Western Medicine joined the Hunan project in offering vegetarian hospital meals, calling itself China's first "vegetarian hospital."

Xing, who now considers herself a pretty good vegetarian chef, suggests beginners could start with vegetarian restaurants before learning how to cook. "There are now more and more specialized vegetarian restaurants that can provide delicious and nutrition-balanced dishes," she says.

Another hurdle for beginners is the potential "anti-social" aspect of their lifestyle, in a culture where it's customary to show "face" to one's dinner guests with a tableful of delicacies, the richer the better. "When I entertain guests, I have to tell them that 'I can't treat you with meat.' It sometimes causes misunderstandings," admits Tang. "It's inevitable. In a family, what if the wife is vegetarian but the husband is not? In the workplace, what if one colleague is vegetarian but not everybody else?"

Xing sees it differently. Being vegetarian, she tells us, introduced her to "a different friendship circle." "We often get together, and

The staff of Yuhuazhai preparing a vegetarian lunch

Hundreds of elderly waiting outside a Guangdong Yuhuazhai
restaurant for a complimentary vegetarian meal

cook vegetarian food by ourselves. Because we share the same beliefs, it's easier to communicate." As for those who can't accept her lifestyle, she admits, "we have gradually grown apart."

With such a rapidly growing market, it's no surprise that the vegetarian food industry is gradually expanding to meet their needs. Media estimates put the number of vegetarian restaurants in China at over 3,000, though the menus of many are beyond the purse of ordinary consumers. Tang agrees that some restaurants are indeed too expensive. "I know someone who runs a vegetarian restaurant where one table of food can reach 10,000 RMB. Some [non-vegetarian] customers treat friends there in order gain 'face,'" he says. "That's just how the restaurant operates: It can stay open just by selling one table per day."

Dr. Xiao doesn't appreciate some of these developments. "I think luxury vegetarian restaurants are going astray," he says. "Only when vegetarian consumption is affordable for ordinary people, can it attract more people to learn about vegetarian diets and adopt a healthier lifestyle. How else can these restaurants stay in business?"

Tang, however, estimates that 70 to 80 percent of the restaurants in this industry are fairly priced. "Most operators are truly willing to promote vegetarian culture out of philanthropic belief." He says these charitable intentions can extend to handing out free vegetarian dishes to people in nursing homes or in need.

The best-known name among Chinese vegetarians is the non-profit Yuhuazhai, a loose federation of charities established (according to business legend) in 2011 in Jiande, Zhejiang province, by an elderly restaurateur who invested his life savings to help save animal lives. Volunteers soon followed and opened their own Yuhuazhai restaurants; by 2017, there were nearly 700

A table of vegetarian dishes, offered by a high-end restaurant in Kunming, Yunnan province, is priced at 160 RMB, or about 25 USD kitchens called Yuhuazhai nationwide.

With the help of social workers and volunteers, Yuhuazhai has given out over 580 million free meals without any coordination, economic interest, or real affiliation among all the branches—not even a registered trademark. According to Southern Weekly, the earliest founders of Yuhuazhai discussed the latter issue, but decided that it was unlikely that a corporate interest would risk sullying their own image by stealing a charitable icon.

Yuhuazhai's success has filled Tang and his followers with confidence, but they acknowledge it's just the beginning. Tang envisages a future with vegetarian schools, workplaces, and nursing homes. He even has a philosophy for vegetarianism, reinterpreted from a verse of the *Bhagavad-Gita* in which Krishna exhorts his followers to neither "trouble other people nor be troubled by them."

"Do not trouble living things, nor be troubled by living things," Tang recites. Or, perhaps more appositely: "You are what you eat."
- Sun Jiahui (孙佳慧)

Originally published in May 2018

Mouth of the Clouds

Once neglected in Chinese cookery, Yunnan food
now thrives by emphasizing what other provinces lack

"When the winter sun of Yunnan floods the whole hill with light," wrote British consul George Litton, surveying China's most ethereal province in 1903, "the view of forest and mountain is so superb that it's easy to believe that a spot so conspicuous, so accessible and so beautiful, must have attracted the religious devotion of men from the time when they were first moved by the conception of the spiritual or the sublime."

This was a strange interlude for Litton's field report, which was otherwise filled with tables and tedious tattle about the economy and road conditions of China's southwestern frontier. But according to Zhang Yingfei, head chef at the Yunnan provincial government restaurant in Beijing, Yunnan always has that effect on people. "The rest of China used to think of us as a backwater—and the food as unsophisticated," he says. "Then as tourism developed, everyone heard about how wonderful it was, and they started wanting a sample of Yunnan in their hometowns."

Evocatively named—Yunnan means "South of the Clouds"—and boasting some of China's best-preserved natural scenery, the province is still not above using artificial means to boost its already considerable charm. In 2003, the prosaic Zhongdian county was renamed Shangri-la after James Hilton's classic novel; back in 1996, after an earthquake, officials in the city of Lijiang displayed unusual foresight in requiring the old city quarters to be rebuilt according to the traditional architectural style of the Naxi minority. Both places now regularly top domestic tour-destination rankings in China.

Also China's most ethnically diverse province, located on a cultural crossroads of East Asia, Southeast Asia, and the Tibetan Plateau, Yunnan appears to thrive by emphasizing its differences—a formula now being applied to popularize its cuisine.

"The one word I'd use to describe Yunnan food is 'ecological'—the ingredients tend to be organic or particular to its region, and we emphasize its freshness and natural flavor in cooking," Zhang says. "As people are concerned with food safety these days, that's a great selling point."

Aside from the perception of freshness, however, even Zhang is hard pressed to name any single feature that summarizes the appeal of Yunnanese food. There are around 10 sub-regions within the province, and around 25 ethnic minority groups—seven with their own autonomous regions—scattered across a geography encompassing both jungle and plateau. There are also influences and ingredients from neighboring regions like Sichuan, and countries like Myanmar and Thailand. The result is that "Dian cuisine" (滇菜), called after the ancient name for the province, is not among China's traditional "Eight Great" regional food systems;

Fresh mushrooms are synonymous
with Yunnan cooking

some natives even argue there is no such single cuisine.

Lu Jing, a young Yunnan architect who moved to Beijing after graduation, is one. "Because there are so many ethnic groups, there are many food cultures in Yunnan," she says. But that, she argues, is actually a point in its favor compared to other Chinese regions. "Foods from Yunnan encompass all the flavors—sweet, sour, bitter, spicy, salty, fresh, and raw. Bitter, especially, is something you rarely find in other [Chinese] food cultures, as are the raw, seasonal ingredients that you can only eat at a particular time of year."

Then, of course, there are the mushrooms, arguably Yunnan's most famous (and certainly priciest) ingredient. According to Lu, "Every year, we hear news reports of people taken to the hospital because they've been poisoned by wild fungi, which they eat in order to hallucinate"—yet another nod to the Yunnan travel experience, given the province's reputation in its border regions, close to the Golden Triangle of drug trade—"or because it's so fresh." Yunnan produces around 250 species of wild mushrooms, around two-thirds of all edible types of fungi in China, and "wild Yunnan fungi"-themed restaurants can be found in some Chinese cities, safely serving creative, exotic mushroom-based dishes for inexperienced foragers to enjoy.

Urbanites' taste for the ecological have created a feedback loop with the local tourism industry. In recent years, organic farms and rural markets in Yunnan have become attractions in their own right, especially where the mushrooms are to be found. In August, a record number of tourists from around the country as well as local buyers gathered in Nanhua county, a self-styled "Kingdom of Wild Mushrooms," where 1,008 tons of fungi were transacted in the first week of the month. In the east of the province, the

PHOTOGRAPH BY VCG

Farmer's markets selling fresh mushrooms draw foodies from around the country to Yunnan

town of Longpeng has been developing a mushroom-based tourism industry complete with an annual mushroom culture festival since 2012.

High-end travel companies based in cities have also begun offering culinary tours that bring Chinese and international travelers to interact with the food producers in the province. At Beijing's WildChina, founded by Harvard-educated Yunnanese-American Mei Zhang, customers experience boutique hotel stays and private driving tours along with activities like making cheese with Yunnan farmers and picking tea leaves, which, according to company marketing manager Emma Clifton, provides an "immersion" in local culture using food as the icebreaker: "In the comfort of their kitchen, Yunnanese people open up and have so many stories to tell."

Those without the time or resources for immersing themselves have make do with elements of Yunnan now creeping into China's cities. "National chains based on Yunnan cuisine are doing extremely well, and we're finally moving beyond the perception that Yunnan cuisine is only 'crossing the bridge rice noodles,'" Chef Zhang says, referencing a famous dish in which rice noodles are cooked beneath a layer of oil. At Yun Hai Yao, a "viral restaurant" popular in Chinese malls, wait-staff who sport the silvery jewelry of ethnic minorities are as much part of the marketing as the food. Meanwhile, metropolitan Shanghai has given birth to the so-called "Lijiang themed" restaurant—small diners catering to a younger market, filled with books and wooden tables evocative of the cafes their millennial customers likely encountered while backpacking around Yunnan itself. Yunnan cuisine is also said to be the food group with the greatest of number of appearances on the CCTV food and travel program *A Bite of China* (《舌尖上的中国》).

Chef Zhang believes it's not just the clientele who benefit from this fever for all things Yunnan. "Yunnan people are stereotyped as 'homebodies'—when you've got everything you need in this province, so many different kinds of foods and geographies, why would you ever want to leave?" he wonders. "Now our chefs are taking notice of the interest in Yunnan, and confident to take our products abroad. That can only make Yunnan food more innovative, and inspire us more." - Hatty Liu

Originally published in November 2017

PHOTOGRAH BY ZHANG DEMENG [张德萌]

Yunnan cuisine emphasizes
freshness corresponding with its
natural scenery

Chapter Three: Housing

"How I wish I could have ten thousand houses,
to provide shelter for all who need it!"

- Du Fu, "My Cottage Unroofed by Autumn Gale"

Nail 'Hood

In a Beijing village, a community of strivers clings to a doomed existence

For Beijingers, the spring of 2018 will likely be remembered as the season of the bricks.

The building of the Great Walls of Gentrification has blocked off—or knocked down—many of the city's mom-and-pop businesses. Yet while progress marches on, the neighborhood of Huashiying (化石营 , literally "Barracks of Fossils"), also known as Guandongdian (关东店) after the nearby thoroughfare, clings improbably to a precarious existence in the shadow of some of the city's most iconic structures.

Despite an imminent demise reported as far back as 2008—when the government made the eradication of improvised buildings and makeshift utilities, known as "shed areas" (棚户区), an urban priority—this warren of shanties, shops, and local culture persists, wedged awkwardly near Beijing's Eastern Third Ring and the gleaming steel and glass of the Central Business District (CBD).

And the survival of central Beijing's last urban village seems even more impressive as the forces of modernity and order rip the heart from the hutong of Dongcheng and backstreets of Chaoyang. But for how long?

Only a few hundred meters across at its widest point, Huashiying is a throwback neighborhood, a window into a not-so-recent past when Beijing accommodated both monumental modern architecture and vibrant local neighborhoods. It is also the kind of organic community as equally reviled by overzealous urban planners in China as romanticized by visitors from afar.

It is an impromptu community of improvised buildings and makeshift utilities. Electric and cable lines crisscross overhead, connecting buildings with hastily rigged boxes which would defy code even in China. "Water bladders," colored black to attract the sun's heat, adorn rooftops, their nozzles dangling through windows and home-drilled apertures to provide at least a semblance of indoor plumbing and hot water to the building's residents.

Formerly occupied by the 3501 Clothing Factory, the neighborhood is ostensibly still home to its retired workers. However, almost all the rooms and shops are sublet to migrants from China's interior. This is the turn-of-the-millennium Beijing that planners are working hard to eradicate: the Anhui auntie with the clothing store; the girls from Dongbei in the sketchy barbershop; the guy from Hebei and his fruit stand.

These neighborhoods, whether established in alleys or inside metropolitan blocks of a more recent vintage, have long been the first stop for rural workers seeking a better life in the capital. They were—and, to the extent allowed in today's capital, still are—footholds for dreamers and the desperate alike to build a future in

Street side vendors, increasingly rare in Beijing's center, line
the alleys, offering low-cost necessities for residents

one of the most dynamic capitals in the world.

But those dreams grow in grime. As with the hutong
neighborhoods of Beijing's old inner city, life in Huashiying is
one of privation. Public bathrooms are a throwback, and not
in a pleasant way, to a time when restrooms looked like the
scatological apocalypse of the Ragnarök, as imagined by Jackson
Pollock.

Rows of old-world brick houses in the center, formerly the
factory's dormitories, function as anchors for the makeshift (and
likely illegal) structures surrounding them. Inside, dark staircases
wind past open doors. Swallows nest between floors, venturing
out, like their human neighbors, in ever-expanding sorties to
bring back life's necessities. Huashiying is a convenient nesting
spot, near enough to one of Beijing's ever-increasing epicenters of
prosperity yet tolerant of all, regardless of means. There are few

PHOTOGRAPHS BY YU BIRUI [俞必睿]

Huashiying is one of the
last urban villages inside of
Beijing's Third Ring Road

quarters in downtown Beijing willing to allow nesting birds in the apartment hallways. The same could be said about affordable housing for the capital's ever-fluctuating migrant population.

But life goes on. In the evening, the streets come alive; people wait until the last possible moment to return to dark and dreary rooms. Children play outside, dodging carts and bicycles. Men smoke and drink, green bottles emptied of cheap beer lying by their feet like fallen soldiers. Young women gossip in doorways, glancing furtively at male passersby.

From above, one can see buildings crowded together in improbable geometries. A sign in the alley leading into the neighborhood warns of fumes from unsafe methods of heating; one fears what a single match might do. Amid the jumble, a lone tree rises from a roof, the surrounding shanties built tightly around the trunk, the roots burrowing into the foundation. China is famous for its "nail houses" (钉子户), lone holdouts against demolition, sticking up despite attempts to tear them down. The tree is a poignant metaphor for the whole block, a "nail tree" at the heart of a "nail neighborhood."

"There's a rough quality," says Jens Schott Knudsen, an attorney and photographer who has lived near Huashiying for five years. "But you get a sense that it's a real community." Knudsen's photographs capture the stark contrasts of Beijing's sometimes-haphazard development. "You have these shantytowns, and in the background is some of the most expensive real estate in the city."

Beijing's urban planners certainly have Huashiying in their crosshairs, yet it's not entirely clear why nobody has pulled the trigger. Local scuttlebutt ranges from the area benefiting from the patronage (or at least the patience) of an influential landowner, to the neighborhood's faintly preposterous reputation as a place for powerful men to quietly stash mistresses. A more likely

Ramshackle spaces offer affordable rent for local business, like this key-cutting and shoe-repair workshop explanation is that the land has simply become too expensive to develop.

The 0.01 square-kilometer CBD plot on which Beijing's tallest skyscraper, the China Zun Tower, is currently nearing completion was purchased by the CITIC Group for an astonishing 6.3 billion RMB; that was in 2010. In 2016, China Real Estate News reported that "Century City," a complex of shops, offices, and high-end apartments, would be built over Huashiying.

Just untangling ownership could prove a lengthy obstacle. In 2011, developers sued disgruntled Tsinghua University faculty members who declined an offer of 2.4 billion RMB to vacate a campus in the CBD, even after the university approved the deal. The same year, new regulations on urban development banned expropriations unless they were for "the public good," effectively making private projects like Century City illegal.

At one of Huashiying's many cheap eateries, the staff speculate about the future. "So many of Beijing's neighborhoods have been demolished," says one. "Someday this will be too. But nobody knows when. It's how it is in Beijing right now."

Like their brick homes, Huashiying's older residents are made of sturdier stuff. "We're the original houses in the neighborhood—they want to move us, but they can't afford it," says Ms. Li, who lived in the neighbourhood for half a century.

She has family all over the city, but doesn't foresee herself leaving. "Dongdaqiao [bus terminal] is right next to us, and I can go anywhere from here," she says. "This wasn't always so developed, but then they built the skyscrapers they covered us up—so we became the 'ugly' parts."

Eventually, this heart of Beijing is expected to serve as the jewel at the center of Jing-Jin-Ji (京津冀), a centrally planned megalopolis

Huashiying's proximity to Beijing's CBD provides a striking visual contrast which will combine the capital with the nearby city of Tianjin. The surrounding countryside of Hebei (the 'Ji,' after one of the province's old names) will sprout communities intended to satisfy the residential, commercial, and industrial demands of the region.

In this vision of a well-regulated urban space—population 80 million or, to put it in other terms, Germany—Beijing's city center will be a "political and cultural zone." Nobody really knows what that means, and the municipal government is being vague on the particulars, perhaps deliberately so. But the mass campaign to brick up and over small businesses, many of which, to be fair, were operating without business licenses or in illegal spaces, suggests it will be, above all, an orderly city.

In the battle between organic—and possibly messy—local culture and the state's relentless fetishization of a sanitized modernity, it seems depressingly clear that Beijing will indeed become a cleaner, more orderly and tidy, but altogether less interesting city.

The denizens of Huashiying do not seem to worry much about forces beyond their control. Several said simply that they don't know when they will be forced to move, but they're expecting the worst.

"It's hung on for so long," says Knudsen, "But it's hard to imagine where the city's going now that it can possibly last much longer." Until that time comes, this tiny urban village endures, an inconvenient reminder of Beijing's diverse past, with little hope of inclusion in its brave new future. - Jeremiah Jenne, with contributions from Hatty Liu and Liu Jue (刘珏)

Originally published in July 2017

The Life Relocated

The unique, inventive lifestyle of residents
moved to make way for modernity

Every half hour, every weekend, the Wuqing high speed railway station fills to bursting point with newly arrived passengers. It's a 20-minute trip on the bullet train from Beijing, after which a flyover pass decorated with Romanesque statues channels the passengers over to "Florentia Village," the biggest outlet mall in northern China.

Built with an investment of one billion RMB, the complex is meant to resemble a "sixteenth century Italian town," with its winding alleyways, a "Roman Square," and an artificial river complete with gondolas. Middle-class shoppers pack the alleyways and stream into their favorite designer shops—Gucci, Prada, and Coach. In 2014, a new shopping center "Venice City" sprang up right beside "Florentia." Under and beyond these monuments to consumerism is the ghost of communities that vanished to make way for modernity—the specter at the food court.

For outsiders, the mall is perhaps the only major attraction of Wuqing. Administratively belonging to Tianjin Municipality, Wuqing district is only 60 kilometers away from Beijing's Fifth Ring Road. Wuqing's governmental website prides itself on its location as "at the very heart of the Beijing-Tianjin-Hebei area."

Compared to other Chinese towns of its size, Wuqing is surprisingly clean and well-maintained; the roads are wide and bordered by well-kept lawns, bushes, and trees of different hues. Everything here—roads, lawns, communities, factory buildings, and office buildings—seem to sprawl endlessly into an overwhelmingly expansive, well-planned, and surreal materialist paradise. However, when one leaves Florentia Village, the facade gives way to a sparsely populated rural town of high rises.

"Ever since 2000, Wuqing has taken urbanization as its development strategy," the district's website claims triumphantly. "Over the past few years, Wuqing dismantled over 5 million square meters of villages, which contained over 100 streets. Over 100,000 residents were turned into urban residents, and their identity, lifestyle, and administration have been fundamentally changed."

The government does not mention how many villages were dismantled or what their names were; rather, they are looked upon at a macro level—streets and square meters to be carved up for profit—a good argument to be sure but one that is never had: the urbanization of rural areas. As the process of urbanization is pushed triumphantly onwards, it becomes increasingly clear that it is presented as a half-told story, with entire communities gone in a flash.

"There were 16 villages," says 49-year-old Li Shuling positively. For the past two years Li has worked the night shift at Yonghe

Real estate developments spring up on land that once held villages and their people

PHOTOGRAPHS BY WANG KUNLUN (王昆仑)

A village remains on the edge of the Wuqing "urbanized" area; the red characters advertise gravestone inscription services

Tianjin's Florentia Village is a tourist attraction as well as a housing development

King, a Chinese fast food franchise. She is petite, energetic, and like most villagers she gets her information through gossip. "The village Florentia Village is built upon was called Liangzhuang. My village was called Danangong." Danangong literally means the "big south palace," a rather grand name for a village that could be built over without anyone noticing. "Now all the villagers of the 16 villages are concentrated in three residential complexes—the Xin Community, the He Community, and the Jing Community."

These three communities are known as "relocation apartments" (回迁房), and they are massive. Each community consists of 81 buildings that look exactly the same, block after block of exactly the same structures. For these originally rural residents, merely picking their home out of the sprawling identical landscape seems a daunting task.

Liu Guihua now works as a custodian for her own block. She protested fiercely when her son tried to persuade her to move into their new apartment on the 17th floor of the new community. Her biggest fear was that she might never learn how to use the elevator, and this was not an uncommon fear among her neighbors. In the humble beginnings of this burgeoning community, it was quite common for a tan-faced, middle-aged man to rush in, look the button board up and down, and anxiously and helplessly ask: "Is it going up or down?"

But, now in their third year of residence, most of the patrons can manage quite well, and many appreciate the merits of life in a building. The heating system and the sewage system delight everyone who had varied experiences with both in their previous accommodations; heating a high-ceilinged village home was almost impossible, and many of their toilets were built at the other end of their yards without proper (or sometimes any) sewage treatment infrastructure.

Wuqing is a town built for cars, and outside these ad hoc communities the roads are wide and bare; no restaurants, no convenience stores. However, those with a bit of business nous quickly started to make a living by selling things from their apartments, and one can get everything they need from these makeshift home stores without ever leaving the community: buying vegetables, renovation services, hairstyling, and more. It appears that, in those listless, identical buildings, a new community has evolved; a self-sufficient organism. They know where to buy vegetables, pancakes and buns, where the barber and the hardware store is, where one can buy curtains. The stores never have signs, but the villagers know them by heart; and when they do get confused, they just need to go into the elevator, which is coated in layer after layer of handwritten numbers and addresses—a sort of community all-in-one yellow pages and information desk.

Despite their surprising and inventive evolution in this new life, the villagers often feel fundamentally frustrated. What bothers Li most is that now every household locks its doors. As she speaks, everyone around nods gravely, sharing the same antipathy of closed doors in the corridors of their residential flats.

Back in the village, their houses were a source of pride, a way to show off their relative wealth and success—personal projects to make their home and community a better place. People never closed their gates as long as someone was home, and when you wanted to visit someone, you just went in. The residents claim gossip is their greatest pastime and that they don't quite agree with or understand all this need for privacy. And while this sounds very much like the complaints of nosy old women looking out their windows and spying on their neighbors, it is and was important to them to visit openly and conveniently to exchange the freshest eggs, vegetables, and rumors.

"Everyone was welcome anytime. But now every household locks their doors, and I have to make phone calls when I just want to have my daily chat with a friend." Li says, "It's a good thing that nowadays mobile phones can connect us very easily; when you lose something, you always get something in compensation, right?"

As a result of this newfound isolation, the lobby on the ground floor has become a sort of town hall. It is always packed, and the regulars take along stools and fans and spend most of their day there. When asked why they do not prefer to stay at home, the answer is uniform: "It's suffocating inside."

Urban residents are used to such isolation from cradle to grave, but to the villagers it is still a new, difficult strain. Everyone adapts to this new way of life differently, but it is hardest for the older generation. Liu Guihua's son believes the high-rise life drove his grandmother to an early grave. "She was very unhappy in her few last days," he recalls. "No one is home because now there are no fields; the family members have to go out and get jobs. She was so desperately lonely and there was no one to turn to. If she had lived in a village she could still attend to her garden, but here she was locked up in the apartment—nowhere to go and nothing to do. She had cancer, and her condition deteriorated very quickly."

In a community that houses tens of thousands of people, death is quite a regular occurrence. Sometimes, they say, there is a funeral almost every week.

In rural areas, funerals are not occasions for mourning and grieving; indeed, they are more like festivals. Just like the height of their houses, the lavishness of the funeral represents the family's status. It's a necessary vanity that no one in the village, including the educated young people, questions. The funerals involve abundant feasts and everyone is on the guest list, a party complete with elaborate decorations, professional mourners, crying, singing, and collapsing on the stage, while the relatives crack sunflower seeds and chat merrily. There are singers crooning "country rock" and dances featuring young and sometimes scantily-clad female dancers.

In 2015, news agencies reported that some funerals in China's countryside featured strippers and caused quite a sensation; but this has actually been quite common for a while, and few in the community bat an eyelash at the thought. The motive behind the shows is less that of eroticism and more one of status, as a bigger crowd for the funeral means more prestige for the family.

Whereas the old villages used to hold the funeral rituals at a home or in a yard, now they take place at the entrance of the community, pretty much the only place with enough cleared land to accommodate the services. The coffin is stationed under one marquee, while the guests dine under another. When night rolls around—what with the pounding music and dancing girls—the crowd is certainly bigger than what they might have drawn in the good old days.

However, even this is not to last. The government built a grand funeral parlor in 2015 and has requested that villagers stop holding funerals in front of the community gates; if they comply, then they get a subsidy of 3,000 RMB. The locals happily cooperated, trading their dancing girls and revelry for a spacious dining room.

When asked how she likes the relocated life in general, Li is hesitant: "My life is...okay...The pressure is greater. When we were in the village and had fields, although farming was never profitable, at least we didn't need to worry about food and housing. You can be quite carefree living on a minimum of expenses.

"But now, living in the building, we have to get hired, earn money, and everything—water, electricity, food—cost money. On the other hand, the government bought everyone insurance, and there was the relocation compensation. It's more pressure, but well, I can only accept it."

In 2014, China's urban population constituted over 54 percent of the nation's population, a remarkable rise considering that it was 19 percent at the beginning of the reform and opening-up period in 1980, and only 35 percent in 2008. China is obviously being urbanized at a stunning speed, and over the past six years, more rural residents have become urban household registration holders than in the previous three decades.

In official reports and analyses, this should be a good thing. Urbanization is often coupled with economic potential, social mobility, and sustainable development. A government paper even proposed that to maintain China's stability, over 70 percent of the population has to be urbanized before 2050. As such, residents in these rural areas ripe for relocation must coalesce into what every newspaper in the land claims is the tide of history.

However, there are the King Canutes of the relocation world who refuse to, or simply can't, accept the status quo; village life is the only life for them. In the Xin Community, people often gossip about their two well-known resident eccentrics. Perhaps the most interesting is an elderly woman in her 50s—she wore her gray hair in two braids and was often seen putting animal feed in the sun to dry. Her neighbors often gossiped about the horrible

Middle-class shoppers swarm
Florentia Village, often unaware
of the people displaced for their
shopping sprees

smells emanating from her apartment, and one autumn night in 2014, the neighbors finally called the cops to deal with the stink. It turned out that she had been raising sheep, chickens, and dogs in her apartment, in addition to hoarding. It took three trucks to ship out the garbage in her rooms.

The other odd-man-out in the community is a physically handicapped victim of polio who transports himself on a wheeled board with the assistance of his mentally challenged wife. He still fetches water from a river running close to the community for cooking and washing, and keeps patches of vegetables by roadsides; he has never paid a single water bill.

While there are woeful tales of inability to adapt, they seem to evaporate under the bright sun. The town, although near Beijing, is cleaner, neater, and not as hazy. It evades the common mistakes often seen in China's urbanization—weird buildings, bad planning, pollution. The villagers are dealing with their new life, taking the good with the bad, while the town itself can be as international, modern, and urban as it likes. - Ginger Huang (黄原竞)

Originally published in July 2015

Tenant Trouble

A rental business riddled with scams, runaway prices, and toxic chemicals in the walls

When a Beijing woman sued rental agency Ziroom in August 2018, blaming the high levels of formaldehyde in one of its Hangzhou apartments for her husband's death from leukemia, Xue Jing was one of many renters in the capital who saw the news and panicked.

"I bought a DIY testing kit, and it told me there were abnormal formaldehyde levels in my bedroom, so I borrowed a meter and got a reading of 0.23 milligrams per cubic meter," Xue told us, quoting a figure more than twice the national maximum. The carcinogen, commonly found in varnishes and paint used in renovations and furniture by companies like Ziroom, is capped at 0.1 milligrams per cubic meter by Chinese law. "I didn't even know this could happen; the agent never said anything before I moved in."

For those in the know, however, it has long been an open secret that harmful chemicals are present in apartments across China—and that this is only the tip of a toxic iceberg. "Actually, all rentals have formaldehyde levels exceeding the maximum; Ziroom is just the biggest offender, and the unluckiest to have gotten caught," one source within Ziroom's competitor, Xiangyu Apartments, told us on the condition of anonymity.

Once a neglected rung on China's heated property ladder, the country's rental market got a push in late 2017 when President Xi Jinping called for homes to be built for "living in," rather than purchased for speculation. However, as cities and state-owned banks responded by rolling out preferential land-use and lending policies, and developers rush to cash in, the rental sector seems to have not only inherited the home purchase market's boom—but also its issues with speculation, poor regulation, and corruption.

Aside from the August's "formaldehyde-gate," this scandal-ridden year of 2018 saw Ziroom censured again in September for evading responsibility for a hidden camera found in one of its Beijing apartments. Meanwhile, chief competitor Danke Apartments was investigated in May for a "pay-by-month" scheme that resulted in tenants getting signed up for loans without their knowledge, which they repaid in the belief that they were simply making rent each month (Danke also paid landlords monthly, meaning that the agency controlled the equivalent of a year's rent in loans with which to expand their business).

The same practice heralded the October bankruptcy of Shanghai-based Yujian Apartments, which crumbled after taking on too much debt in order to acquire rental properties from homeowners, leaving landlords with unpaid rent and tenants potentially still on the hook for the loans in their name.

All this comes alongside growing anxiety that rents have simply

Beijing renters change homes on average once every 11 months, according to a 2016 study

increased too much, and show no sign of stopping in spite of the blatant disregard to tenants' credit, safety, or health. Among first and second-tier cities, Chengdu and Shenzhen led the price surge, with the average cost of rent increasing 31 and 30 percent, respectively, from 2017 to 2018; in parts of Beijing, rent jumped 10 percent just between June and July of 2018. "Rent prices see astronomical increase; tenants pay with their lives!" shouted the summer's headlines. "Pay the highest price and breathe the most toxic chemicals!"

In August 2018, a Beijing homeowner revealed that an apartment he had planned to rent out for 7,500 RMB (1,000 USD) per month was eventually listed at 10,800 RMB (1,500 USD) per month, after Ziroom and Danke tried to "outbid" each other for the right to lease the unit. More mysteriously, in June, Hu Jinghui, then vice-CEO of real estate agency 5I5J, accused competitors of driving up rent prices and called for government regulation—then abruptly resigned the next day, claiming pressure from Ziroom's parent company Lianjia.

For tenants, it's a depressing cycle of shady bargains, high fees, and not knowing where to turn to help. "All [the help] that the agent gave me were green turnip plants to 'suck up the chemicals,'" Xue complains. "It made me feel very helpless."

Several of Chu Min's roommates were still in their rooms when the demolition crew came one early morning in September.

"I saw a plastic card being slipped inside our door, breaking it open. A member of the residential committee came in, followed by policemen, and a crowd of workers, who said they've come to tear down [illegal] apartment subdivisions," he says. "Some of my roommates, who hadn't gone to work yet, got smothered in falling dust as their walls were knocked down."

For those caught up in the summer's scandals, it may be hard to imagine that "branded apartments" (品牌公寓) such as Ziroom's were once touted as a solution to an abusive industry where experiences like Chu's were the norm. A US-educated "overseas returnee" with no prior experience renting in China, Chu left his first apartment in Beijing because his agent pressured him to pay rent ahead of its due date, and moved into what he believed was a four-bedroom loft. "It got subdivided into nine bedrooms. I'd been completely scammed."

Chu had fallen for a classic bait-and-switch by "shady agents" (黑中介), a term for unlicensed, fly-by-night operators that typically pose as tenants to obtain apartments from homeowners or other agencies, make modifications to the unit, and sublease it, often with various illegal fees tacked on. "In reality, all agents subdivide apartments so they can rent them out for more money," Chu says, "and if I want to move out, they'll say I broke the lease and forfeit my deposit." It's also not clear if Chu would still be on the hook for any loan they took out in his name.

Other underhand ploys involve agents delaying repairs, cutting off utilities, or claiming that the unit will be demolished or repossessed by the owner; tenants are then offered a less attractive apartment, and forfeit their deposits or even rent they'd already paid when they (predictably) refuse to move out. "Then, once they've gotten rid of the tenant, they'll repeat the process with another," says Chu, calling the practice "apartment laundering." When problems arise, unlicensed agents also simply disappear. Their scams are difficult to prosecute because they are considered individual subletters rather than corporate parties under a lease.

Unscrupulous brokers have been a feature of China's real estate history since at least the eighth century—when they were called *yaren* (牙人) and banned from the capital. The modern crisis, though, is related to the building boom that began with the commercialization of China's housing policies in 1994. By 1998, the State Council had formally abolished the Communist housing distribution system, and many cities began to develop their land into new housing projects to boost their GDP and absorb the inflow of rural migrants.

It wasn't long before collectivism had swung in favor of a cultural obsession with homeownership, fueled by an economy that offered few other surefire investments or social safety nets. This is especially true in first-tier cities: Home-ownership is usually a prerequisite for obtaining a local household registration (*hukou*), as well as other social resources, such as places at desirable schools. Public housing is also virtually inexistent—instead, almost all new developments are for profit, contributing to runaway price inflation.

There is no official study for the vacancy rates of Chinese apartments—that is, the percentage of purchased properties that are neither occupied nor rented out—though most unofficial studies since 2013 have put the figure between 20 to 30 percent. For absentee landlords, agencies play a crucial role in finding tenants and looking after their spare investment properties. "I'm unable to go deal with the tenants myself, but with an agent, I basically don't have to worry," said Beijing homeowner Mr. Feng, who has since moved back to his hometown of Shenyang, but has no plans on selling.

China lags in providing legal protection for either tenants or landlords; nor are there authorities such as rental boards that deal specifically with rental properties and leases. The obligations of the renter, agent, and landlord to respect their lease are broadly outlined under the PRC's Contract Law. However, no city or province has comprehensively addressed matters such as who is legally entitled to lease or sublease an apartment, what fees they are allowed to collect, and the maximum by which the prices can increase by year.

In this sellers' market, renters feel compelled to pay whatever they are charged, or move out and cut their losses if they're dissatisfied, rather than face the rigmarole of a civil action where the verdict is unlikely to be enforced. Recent graduates, with little money or legal know-how, are especially vulnerable to predatory agents and too-good-to-be-true deals. China's lack of a consumer credit system means that rent is usually paid in three-month

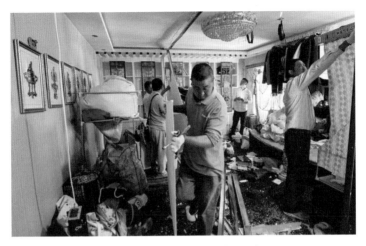

Workers tear down illegal subdivisions that real estate agents
used to convert a living room into two bedrooms

installments or more. Added with the equivalent of at least a
month's rent, each, in agent fees and a deposit, it amounts to a
minimum up-front payment equal to five months' rent before the
tenant even moves in, not counting other miscellaneous fees that
an unlicensed agent may tack on.

"I've looked at better apartments, with [more established
agencies such as] 5I5J, but they ask for *two* months' deposit plus
three months' rent, which is more than I can afford," says Chu.
"Small agencies are my only other option."

In September 2018, he received notice that his third apartment
in Beijing is yet another illegal subdivision scheduled for
demolition, but moving isn't an option. "It could take several
months to get my deposit back, and I can't afford an additional
three months' rent and a deposit on a new place, so I'll stay until
they tear it down—I'll actually lose less that way."

"When I first found a job in Beijing and began looking for an apartment, I thought it was such a mess," Xue recalls. "I met 'professional subletters,' agents posing as owners, shady agents...many apartments had passed through two or three hands [before I saw it], so I thought of trying a 'branded apartment,' where I'd pay more, but gain peace of mind."

After signing her lease with Ziroom, Xue was impressed by the modern furnishings, housekeeping service, and on-call repairs offered by the agency's mobile app. Brands like Ziroom and Danke, along with competitors such as 5I5J's Xiangyu, are positioned as younger, white-collar subsidiaries of their respective parent companies (Danke's is Ziwutong, a Beijing property management firm).

The usual business model of "branded apartments" is to sign landlords for slightly longer leases than the typical letting agency, usually five years, install standardized renovations such as drywall, and furnish to the unit before renting it out at higher prices. Since starting in 2011, Ziroom's main selling point has been a lack of agents (though it employs similar individuals called "stewards") and agent fees (though its "service fee" can be even higher). Pricing is said to be transparent, with monthly rent and amenities spelled out on the agency's app, which acts as a centralized platform for tenants to pay rent and request services.

According to classifieds website 58.com, the branded apartment market saw its sharpest growth in the latter part of 2017, with hundreds of thousands of listings in more than 20 major cities in China. It's not only traditional real estate agencies leaping on the branded bandwagon, but property developers like Vanke, hotels chains like HomeInn, and independent startups. More recently, it has become popular for developers to offload underused hotels, office buildings, and even malls to be redeveloped into "centralized apartments"—whole complexes of studio units and common areas rented out by a single company.

The industry has also attracted high-profile investors: Xiaomi founder Lei Jun invested in both the now-defunct Yujian and You+, a centralized apartment startup, while Tencent has backed Ziroom. International backers are also sniffing around, with US-based Tiger Global Management leading a 70 million USD financing round for Danke in June 2018, and global equity firm Warburg Pincus backing Ziroom and Mofang Apartments.

The summer's scandals were something of a reality check to this industry pile-on, though sharp-eyed renters would have noticed that harmful formaldehyde levels had been reported in Ziroom apartments before. In fact, according to the Jinan Times, there have been 10 previous lawsuits relating to formaldehyde in residential units, none successful, as tenants could not prove that their health problems were directly related to the apartment.

However, after Ziroom took all new apartments offline for a month for third-party air quality inspections following the scandal, many have been quietly put back online as of October—and health and safety issues are being reported again. Branded agents are also not immune to the old trick of subdividing apartments: This past winter, surprised Ziroom and Danke customers in Beijing returned to find their bedroom walls smashed ("They didn't even lock the door after," one complained on Danke's app), part of a citywide crackdown after a deadly fire in Daxing district in November 2017.

"After leaving Danke, I've decided to rent only from individual [landlords]," vows Wang Yi, one of the victims of the agency's monthly loan scheme. Getting out of the brand's shadow is easier said than done, though: Since breaking her lease, Wang has been unable to reach the company to pay back the 700 RMB owed on her balance. "I recently got denied a credit card. I'm worried this will affect my credit permanently."

There are way too many renters with stories to tell," says Liu Ruiting, co-founder of Kan Fang Gou ("Apartment-Hunting Dog"), a self-proclaimed "half charitable, half commercial" startup that grew out of a WeChat account exposing rental horror stories. "In the beginning, we noticed that there were a lot of issues, some of which we experienced ourselves, and created WeChat groups where people could warn each other about shady agents."

Run by teams of volunteers across China, the platform has since branched out to provide a landlord-tenant matching service, an agent blacklist, and free consultation about rental contracts. Its most active features, though, are still the WeChat "complaint groups"—which have become a platform not only for tenants who fell for the same scams to commiserate, but find collaborative solutions.

Chu, who is a member of several such groups, says he has reported agents' bait-and-switch practices to a public security bureau overseeing his neighborhood's "itinerant population," as well as the local residential committee. However, "They kept telling me they have no power of law enforcement, and I was to blame for renting an illegal apartment, which is like buying stolen goods," he says. "It made me feel really angry; I was clearly the victim."

He has also filled out an online complaint with the Ministry

A "mega-complex" outside of Beijing's Fifth Ring Road houses
many renters and transplants in over 9,000 units

of Housing, and is considering going to the industrial and
commercial bureau regarding items in his lease that violate the
Contract Law. "I've been taking pictures of every document I've
signed with [the agents] and preparing to go to court at any time."

Wang is also considering going to the industrial and commercial
bureau. "I heard it's the solution that gives the best results vis-
à-vis the cost." Xue, though, fears that no kind of result can be
worth the time and effort it will require. "I've complained to the
housing ministry, and joined in the WeChat groups, but I'm too
busy with work to pursue it further," she says. "Anyway, all the
institutions I called just kept transferring me."

She now plans to stay out her lease, even renew, if there's no
better option. "By then I'll have already breathed [the chemicals]
for a year and probably inhaled all there is," she half-jokes.

However, remarkably for someone who deals with rental

corruption cases each day, Liu believes the situation is improving. "It's not apparent yet, but the forecast looks good—for example, there's a new law where landlords and agents will have to report the amount they charge to the authorities," she says, referring to a policy unveiled by Zhejiang province on October 19, which also bans hidden loans, makes agencies liable for air quality violations in their apartments, and caps rent increase at 5 percent on average over one year.

In August 2018, Beijing's housing ministry also got the city's top agencies to agree to stop "apartment-bidding," hoping to cool the prices. "In the future, we hope to see improved regulation on how much the agents may charge, and if they obtain property under false pretenses," says Liu.

Wang, similarly, hasn't lost faith in agencies, believing they can correct themselves with better management. "I'd like to try a centralized apartment next; they ought to be easier to supervise."

Chu disagrees. "I no longer have any trust—not for Ziroom, Danke, or anybody," he says. "I don't care how big they get; they're never too big to fail. And then where will I be?" - Hatty Liu, with contributions from Sun Jiahui (孙佳慧)

Originally published in November 2018

Shock of the New

Regional 'new' cities vie for graduates with cushy
offers, but will the 'talent war' end in tiers?

To stay or leave—it's the question many in China's first-tier
cities are asking. Faced with skyrocketing housing prices,
rising expenses, and increasingly fierce competition for jobs,
those living in Beijing, Shanghai, Guangzhou, and Shenzhen are
considering alternative options.

Traditionally, though, there haven't been many: Most second-
and third-tier cities lack the promising work opportunities,
entertainment, and nightlife associated with modern city life, and
well-developed infrastructure to woo the middle class. On social
media, the dilemma has been skewered in a world-weary viral
phrase: "The first-tier cities cannot accommodate my body, while
the lowe-tier cities cannot fill my soul."

Enter the "New First-Tier Cities"—as coined by CBN Weekly
in 2013—hoping to solve the problem. Every year, the magazine
ranks hundreds of Chinese cities' commercial attractions based on

five indicators—concentration of commercial resources, transport links, the "vitality" of citizens, variety of lifestyle, and "flexibility toward the future." Those in the "new first-tier" category—which is positioned between China's four first-tier cities (Beijing, Shenzhen, Shanghai, and Guangzhou) and 30 second-tier cites—are aiming to be the next locus and engine of China's urban growth.

According to CBN's latest rankings, Chengdu, the capital of southwest China's Sichuan province, is the highest-ranked among the 15 New First-Tier Cities, followed by Hangzhou, Chongqing, Wuhan, Suzhou, and Xi'an. Marketing professional Yang Hao, a 30-something who moved to Chengdu from Beijing in 2012, says he's not surprised. "Chengdu is developing very rapidly," Yang reflects. "So much has already changed since I first got here."

In June 2012, Yang was sent on a business trip to Chengdu, where he enjoyed the relaxed pace of life, a far cry from his hectic life in the capital (during which he changed jobs three times in five years). Yang likens Beijing to "a huge machine. Living there, you cannot have your own shape; you can only be forged into whatever shape it needs."

By contrast, he felt that people living in Chengdu do not seem as anxious about the future. "There's just a feeling that no one is going to shove you in the subway."

When his company offered him a new position in Chengdu, Yang accepted it with little hesitation. Though he wouldn't say he was "fleeing" Beijing, Yang recalls never really having a sense of belonging in the city. "In Beijing, almost every day I heard people mention the term '外地人' ('outsider,' those without a Beijing household registration, or anyone not born and raised in the city), but I have never once heard that phrase in Chengdu."

Not only does Chengdu seem more open to outsiders, but the

On a clear day in Chengdu, residents organize an impromptu
tea house in Wangjiang Park

local government has ambitions to attract more to the city. In
2017, the "Plan for Migrants in Chengdu," was released, allowing
people with a bachelor's degree or above, who have committed
to working at least two years for a local company, to apply for a
Chengdu registration, or *hukou*. The city even set up 20 special
hostels, providing seven days' free accommodation for job-seekers.

Yang marvels at how Chengdu has changed over the last
five years. "Following the development process of Beijing. It
is expanding from a First Ring [Road] and a Second Ring all
the way to a Fifth Ring." He admits, though, that the western
city still has a long way to catch up with first-tier metropolises.
Exciting opportunities are not as easy to come by—especially for
his Korean wife. In Beijing, she found camaraderie in Wangjing's
Korea Town, as well as a plethora of work opportunities.

Yet in spite of minor setbacks, Yang and his wife now plan to piggyback on the rise of Chengdu to the very top. "Chengdu is changing...The city recognized that its future development depends on attracting people, or talent."

"What's the most expensive thing in the twenty-first century?" asked the villain in Feng Xiaogang's 2004 movie, *A World Without Thieves*. "Talent!" Fourteen years later, its prophecy has come true. Since 2017, dozens of cities, including several "New First-Tier Cities," have rolled out favorable policies to attract graduates—a "talent-grab war," in the words of Chinese media.

Though each cities' policies vary, they generally focus on issues such as *hukou* and housing subsidies. In 2017, Wuhan, the capital of Hubei province, permitted university graduates to buy and rent at prices 20 percent lower than market rates. That same year, Changsha, capital of Hunan, announced that it would offer housing and living subsidies between 6,000 RMB to 15,000 RMB per year for university degree-holders who could contribute to the city's development.

And in Jiangsu province's capital, Nanjing, holders of bachelor or vocational degrees, overseas returnees, and self-employed graduates were invited to apply for 30-square-meter public rental houses or subsidies between 600 RMB to 1,000 RMB per month.

"In the short term, these policies, like housing subsidies, are attractive, especially in cities with a large amount of universities, like Wuhan and Xi'an," Li Yan, leader of 58 Recruitment Academy, told 21st Century Business Herald.

Tianjin, a municipality near Beijing, upped the ante earlier this year by offering a *hukou* for anyone under 40 with a bachelor's degree, or under 45 with a master's degree, and all who have a PhD; less than 24 hours after the announcement, the municipality was besieged by over 300,000 applications on the app set up for the procedure. In 2017, over 142,000 graduates registered their *hukou* in Wuhan, six times that of 2016, according to Guangming Daily; 245,000 people transferred their *hukou* to Xi'an; and Changsha saw a registered population increase of about 273,000.

In May, a survey carried out by Zhaopin.com, one of China's leading recruitment websites, suggested over 40 percent of graduates in 2018 wanted to work in six of the major New First-Tier Cities—Hangzhou, Chengdu, Chongqing, Tianjin, Nanjing, and Wuhan; about 34 percent had already signed a contract.

Among these cities, Hangzhou is widely considered the most attractive: According to a report from recruitment website Boss Zhipin, nearly 90 percent of graduates from universities in Hangzhou chose to stay after graduation. For every 100 who leave, it's estimated there are 132 graduates settling, a ratio comfortably ahead of other first-tier cities. Hangzhou is also the most popular city among overseas returnees, even outperforming Beijing and Shanghai, according to a report from LinkedIn in 2017.

For many, the charms of Hangzhou are as obvious as the old saying suggests: "There's heaven in the sky, and Suzhou and Hangzhou on Earth." For job-seekers, though, it's Alibaba, and other companies headquartered in Hangzhou's well-developed tech sector, that are the key to this "paradise."

The reason Li Jing (pseudonym) moved from Beijing to Hangzhou was the opportunity to work for the e-commerce giant. When her company was acquired by Alibaba in 2015, the product developer immediately accepted the offer of a new contract. "For me, it was just an opportunity to work in a bigger platform to continue developing my product," says Li. "But my parents were very glad I came to Hangzhou, because they were concerned with Beijing's housing prices."

Alibaba's presence has given Hangzhou the nickname "Capital of E-commerce," and Qdaily reported that over 36 percent of rentals in the city were to IT workers. But while many hope that life in the New First-Tier Cities will be less chaotic and more fulfilling than the old first-tiers, Li's experience suggests this is not necessarily true. She believes her life in Hangzhou is more stressful, even though she earns five times her Beijing salary. "Every weekday, I leave home at 9 a.m. and arrive home at 10 p.m. I also work overtime at weekends.

"In my free time, I need to improve myself," she adds. "In this industry, if you want to catch up with others, you have to work really hard." Li says that current policy incentives are far from enough—high-end, experienced workers are still in short supply. "I never heard of any department in Alibaba without vacancies."

Others disagree. Lu Ming, a scholar from Shanghai Jiao Tong University, believes the policies are intrinsically unfair. "All of these talent-grabbing policies are just using taxpayers' money to subsidize university graduates, who already have the potential to earn high incomes," Lu told the 21st Century Business Herald. "It is not right if cities only try to keep students, while those without a diploma are forced to leave because they cannot access the same public welfare."

Zhang Shuguang, deputy director at the Unirule Institute of Economics, believes that talent-grabbing policies are generally good. "We used to not respect talent," he noted at the 2018 China's Economic Growth and Cycles Summit. However, Zhang warned that there are problems with "the standards that define high-end talent, and the settlement packages...On the one hand, we see governments attracting high-end talent; on the other hand, we also see some local governments evicting low-end labor.

"Talent is multi-faceted," Zhang concluded. "Without the free movement of people, I don't think such policies will produce satisfactory outcomes."

There's also the question of whether the influx into these New First-Tier Cities is sustainable: While Yang felt that one can really "have a life" outside work in Chengdu, Li, in Hangzhou, feels it may soon be time to leave. Although she has already married and bought two apartments in the city, "I can see the 'ceiling' of my career, and if [so]...I don't want to invest all my time and energy on it," Li says, explaining that she feels it is "the right time" to leave. "Many friends feel I can just continue working at Alibaba for the rest of my life, but they don't realize how exhausting that is."

Days after she spoke with us, Li updated her WeChat Moments, announcing that she has quit. She's planning to relocate, perhaps even go abroad to New Zealand. "I do not want to settle down in any specific place now," she tells us, adding perhaps the most significant factor in these decisions, "I think the internet has reduced the regional influence on people's lives." - Sun Jiahui (孙佳慧)

Originally published in July 2018

Chapter Four: Transportation

"Life is like a journey; I too am on my way."

- Su Shi, "Lin Jiang Xian, Send Off Qian Mufu"

Green Train Blues

Ten hours on China's mobile public forum

2:30 p.m., Gubeikou

Train 4471, the daily service from Beijing to Chengde, stops at Gubeikou Pass in the Yan Mountains every afternoon. Rumor has it that it delivers fresh vegetables to a military police contingent nearby. It's a step down from the thousands of soldiers who defended the capital from here against the Japanese in 1933, and much reduced compared to the Ming dynasty, when the scraggy, sun-scorched ramparts of the Great Wall now overlooking the tracks had been the imperial army's last stand before the Beijing city gates.

For the passengers, the doors don't open and there's no way to tell if you're really riding with the border patrol's greens. However, the few minutes the train spends at the pass serve as a convenient visual reminder that you're leaving Beijing and entering the province of Hebei. "We've 'exited the frontier,'" says Mr. Dai, a construction worker seated to my right. He's using an ancient term, *chusai* (出 塞), which in modern Chinese retains all its evocations of exiled politicians, princesses married off to far-off tribes, and poor settlers setting forth into the unknown. But for Dai it actually connotes the opposite. "Once you exit the frontier, you know you're almost home." And suddenly he's smiling, "*finally.*"

Gubeikou is just 140 kilometers northeast of Beijing, but we've been on the road since nine in the morning. That's an average speed of 25 kilometers an hour, one-fourteenth the speed of the Chinese rail system's showpiece high-speed rail. Dubbed "green-skinned trains"(绿皮火车) for their iconic forest green livery and yellow trim, trains like 4471 are, unsurprisingly, living on borrowed time in a country in which rail infrastructure has long been a matter of national pride.

Whereas China's HSR network, the world's longest as of three years ago, gains around 2,000 kilometers of track each year, four out of seven remaining green train services in the Beijing area were phased out at the start of 2017; 4471 is one of the only survivors, and even it has had its schedule reduced. Where these old rattlers are still found, pulling carriages left over from the 1980s, they obey a protocol that the passengers sum up as, "stopping wherever there's a station, standing aside wherever there's a passing train." We literally make way for modernity.

"Why are you on this train?" four young passengers sitting across the aisle (three e-commerce entrepreneurs and an accountant, they introduce themselves) ask me as soon as I sit down. Traveling with a camera, no luggage, and two foreign interns, I am cut out for the HSR's air-conditioned interiors and plush seats. My new

Authorities are repainting new trains with green livery to "remind people of travel," but few authentic 80s green hard-seat trains remain

Attendants are responsible for selling food, checking tickets, and keeping order among the sometimes rowdy passegers; their mood visibly improves as the train nears its destination

companions sport bright colors and collegiate-looking glasses that stand out sharply against the cream carriage walls and faded blue leather benches, whose backs are so perpendicular that they make the sitter hunch. I reply that I like old trains and cheap fares, and pose the question back at them. "All other trains were sold out," they admit.

On a Chinese train you can tell a lot about the travelers simply from what they bring. My friends across the aisle, who are not here by choice, travel with hard-shell suitcases, ornaments on their phones, and a seemingly bottomless supply of dried convenience-store snacks that they bring out one by one. Dai the construction worker, who takes this train every month, brought sunflower seeds and a luggage trolley loaded with variously shaped packages wrapped in plastic bags, suitable for a short visit home.

The baskets of fruit and monstrously large striped sacks belong to a riotous knot of workers seated in the back. Today is the first day of the week-long National Day holidays, the only time apart from the Spring Festival that many migrant workers in China get to visit home; they are a group of mostly strangers who've discovered they hail from the same county and are anointing their new acquaintance with beer, conversation, and a case of yellow apricots that someone has passed around. This hasn't changed throughout the decades on the green-skinned train: On a journey of tens of hours, with no distractions, but close proximity to more individuals than perhaps any other moment in your life, the nation gets together to talk.

9:35 a.m., Beijing

By the time we crawl out of the North Fifth Ring Road, the crowd in the back are in full caucus led by a man surnamed Jiang who, beer in hand, has chosen a topic that perfectly parallels his swinging moods: money. "You can never buy a house in Beijing, a worker like you!" he shouts at another passenger. "Better come home and build a nice house."

By the time I'm shuffled into their midst by way of the roulette-like seat-changes typical of a sold-out train, Mr. Jiang has started on the fields of wheat outside the window. "See that? Frozen to death. Farming is too expensive, that's why I haven't done it in 10 years," he says. Then he eyes the camera in my hand. "Are you a journalist? Forget Chengde, come to my village, we've got everything journalists want to see: houses falling down, paralyzed people on the bed…like my oldest brother, he's a vegetable now, because healthcare is too expensive."

Across from me a woman surnamed Cao takes up the thread. "It's so expensive to start a lawsuit," she says, continuing an earlier conversation with Jiang's sister-in-law, Ms. Tan. "You can sue all your life and never win, and then if the other side has money, they'll pay someone to get revenge."

Someone recommends contacting a TV station—"These days, the boss would never dare to withhold pay from migrant workers, because they'll get exposed"—and by the time I'm shuffled back to Dai and our new seatmate, Mr. You, the two of them are complaining about the price of food on the train. "See that beer on the trolley? It's 10 *kuai*. Even bottled water is 5 *kuai*. In the store you used to find beer for 6 *kuai* but it's all 10, 15 now," You says, and Dai replies, chuckling, "Instant noodles are still 6 *kuai*; it's probably the only thing that hasn't changed." The hot water is still free as well, warmed by the train's 80s-built coal stoves that also heat the carriages in winter and make everyone's nose itch.

The green train itself, it's soon apparent, is the other exception to the everything-is-expensive clause to life in modern China. "We always take this train home, when we do go home," Tan tells me aside, almost apologetically, as behind her, the crowd begins comparing their houses in the village have appreciated in value. "Time is no consequence, it's cheap"—around 18 RMB to their hometown in Hebei, as in the 80s, but 110 RMB to go the same distance by HSR—"and that's good enough for people like us."

At one point in China's recent past this was, by necessity, good enough for everyone else as well. Commercial rail travel began in earnest in China after the 1978 reforms loosened the restrictions of the household registration (*hukou*) system and university education resumed after a 10-year interruption by the Cultural Revolution. Students and rural workers alike began flooding into Chinese cities to seek new opportunities. However, with the reduction in state funding to several sectors of the economy, rail development included, it was estimated that Chinese trains in this period ran at 50 percent over capacity at all times—100 percent at peak periods.

For passengers, this meant carriages crammed full to the doors, forcing ticket-holders to board through the windows against the attempts by other long-suffering passengers to push them back out. A trip from Beijing to Shanghai, now five hours by HSR, could take 40 hours; passengers sat on the seat-backs and tables and slept under seats or on luggage racks, where farmers might also keep livestock.

However, the overcrowded train carriage—crammed with disparate segments of the population, journeying for days on in the neutral hinterlands in between cities—was also a social space unlike any other at a time in China when collectivist ideals were

PHOTOGRAPH BY HATTY LIU

Jiang, his son, and Tan all travel home from Beijing whenever
their schedules permit—that is to say, just twice a year

being abandoned and the foundations for today's wealth gap
were laid. For all intents and purposes, there was (and is) just one
class on the green train; a near-mythical "hard berth" class was
said to exist, but tickets were always sold out or appropriated
by those with connections. Everyone else, from student to
entrepreneur to peasant-turned-migrant worker, did time together
in the "hard seat" carriage.

As the generation that came of age in the post-reform era is fond
of recalling, it was smelly, chaotic, and they wouldn't want it
back under any terms compared to the spaciousness and genteel
calm of the HSR—but it was also a formative social experience,
undergone collectively, made possible by people from many walks
of life leaving home and their prescribed social roles for the first
time. No one with rudimentary people skills was without partners
for a card game or offers of food to share.

5:25 p.m., Naohaiying Station

A public space made up of diverse social interests, almost by default, becomes a political space as well. In modern China, where the "mass line" model of political participation has mandated that grievances be addressed to the Party and change to come only through the Party apparatus, it's sometimes said that only three forums still exist where individuals can vent their criticism. Before there was the internet and the heated political debates that are reputed to take place inside the nation's taxis, there was the train.

Qing dynasty reformer Kang Youwei (康有为), in as early as the late nineteenth century, had singled out the railroad a major component in his ultimately failed proposals for "strengthening the nation"—it "lent itself to connecting language, likewise customs," he wrote, and would lead to the "transmission of wisdom." Ironically, it would be in 1966, when the nation was on the verge of breakdown, that the railroad was first mobilized to a definite political aim. During the "Great Linkage" movement of the Cultural Revolution, when Red Guards could ride the rails for free, millions of youths traveled to attend rallies in Beijing and then to undergo "re-education" in the countryside. It presaged the travel boom of the 80s both in that it was the first time the post-1949 rail system saw significant ridership, and that carriage capacities were stretched beyond limit.

Packed in for days on end with their peers from around the country, Red Guards sang revolutionary songs, fought, and tried their best to study the masses they met on the train or saw outside. But they also traded stories, played cards, and flirted like youths away from home for the first time; as historian and former Red

Guard Zhu Xueqin recalled in an essay, the overcrowded carriage gave couples the ideal excuse to sit in each other's laps.

As the student generation of the 80s grew up and grew rich side-by-side with the Chinese economy, now enjoying a great variety of train speeds, leg room, and privacy levels commensurate to their individual needs and achievements in the capitalist lottery, it's the migrant class that has remained on the green train, and unclear what effect their discussions can achieve.

As we inch closer to the workers' final destination of Longhua county, Hebei, the strident mood of the carriage as we exited the frontier dampened into a discussion of Su Laosan, literally "Su the Third," a cult figure whose name only I appear to not know. He's the host of Hebei TV's rural channel, a folk hero who accepts people's invitations to come and do exposés on their villages' problems. Inspired by my camera, which has turned out to be the most revealing object on this journey after all, they are wondering how they can get their stories told.

Tan doesn't believe they can. "He's just a hotline. You can call to complain, and he'll send a journalist over, but you don't know what will happen after that, what they'll do 'above,'" she says, referring by shorthand to the bureaucratic layers through which all national policy and funding, however initially promising, are filtered and diluted by the time it reaches their level.

"'The sky is high and the emperor is far away,'" Cao quotes.

"It's not the hard work that's the problem, as long as they treat you right, you know?" Tan says after a pause. "You're happy to work long hours"—or go home only twice a year—"when others are respectful to you, pay attention to your needs."

At a 30-minute stop at Naohaiying, a station surrounded by wheat fields near the end of the journey, we're let out for a walk on the platform, and my fellow travelers discuss house prices again with Mr. He, the lone stationmaster. He seems pleased by the company for as he tells me, beaming, we're the only passenger train that stops here all day. "Not even the return train comes here." In January 2017, three month after my journey, Naohaiying was removed from Train 4471's schedule; no passenger trains now stop at the station in the wheat fields at all, and I wonder if the space for a spontaneous public forum in China has grown smaller still.

6:15 p.m., Longhua, Hebei

"It's a good way to meet people, to unwind," Tan says of the green train. "We started talking and found out we're all from the same place, and we've been talking ever since."

Perhaps only during peak periods like the Spring Festival or National Day holiday—when, as in the 80s, the green train might be the only choice—can you "meet" people on the train still: young entrepreneurs huddled over their screens until you draw them into conversation, someone with a camera who might be able to tell your story.

I had not sat down among the workers in the back for long before I'm asked for contact details. The few business cards I had are snatched up. "Maybe your village will end up on TV tomorrow," Jiang jokes to each person in turn, though I've told him several times, I don't work in TV. A woman sitting nearby, whom I've never spoken to, comes over and takes my last card, then hands it back after reading.

"Maybe it won't make any difference," Cao's seatmate, Mr. Li, suddenly pipes up. He's holding the card and looking at me, though his phrasing is strictly third-person. "Even if we tell journalists what's going on, and they put us on TV, maybe nothing will happen. Right?"

I think I'm supposed to contradict him.

At Longhua, the train all but empties. The young entrepreneurs, Jiang, and the others file past me, and in the flurry of goodbyes, of everyone fetching their own luggage and calculating the taxi fare home, they've all become like strangers again.

But before all of the passengers have gone, I look up, and the woman who returned my card earlier is back. Smiling slightly, and still without saying a word, she takes the last card from my hands and hurries out the door. - Hatty Liu

Originally published in March 2017

承 德 北京北
CHENGDE BEIJINGBI

Passengers get to stretch their legs
during the long stops that slow trains
make in country stations

Third Wheels

In spite of crackdowns, the motorized tricycle is an
essential transportation tool in urban and rural China

"In order to celebrate the 24th birthday of the People's
Liberation Army, to remember forever their heroic struggles
on Jinggangshan Mountain," announced acting PLA chief of
staff Nie Rongzhen on August 3, 1951, unveiling five motorized
bicycles, "this military-use heavy machinery push-bike shall be
named 'the Jinggangshan.'"

They may not have sounded particularly exciting, in Nie's
formulation, but the Jinggangshan would prove to be a triumph
for modern Chinese engineering.

Lacking experience in manufacturing motorbikes, workers at
the PLA No. 6 Automobile Plant had reverse-engineered the
Jinggangshan by taking apart and copying the pieces of a German
Zündapp K500 motorcycle. By 1954, though, the military was
already demanding Jinggangshan brand three-wheelers in order
to transport more people—and the bombastic original two-wheeler

went out of production just a year later, as the motorized tricycle sputtered its way into Chinese transportation history.

These lessons in improvisation, adaptation, and understanding a vast country's logistical needs are still relevant today: According to the Chinese Association of Automobile Manufacturers, 8 to 9 million electric-powered tricycles were manufactured in China in 2017, and 1.7 million powered by diesel, not counting push-tricycles illegally upgraded with motors by their owners. These vehicles serve important functions in both town and countryside, ferrying people and produce, as well as over 4 billion courier parcels per year—but also pose problems of safety, congestion, and unsightly aesthetics on China's increasingly crowded roads.

The tricycle wasn't always a nuisance. In 1964, the Shanghai Motorcycle Factory was already making compact motorized three-wheelers, with an enclosed, bullet-like body, for passenger transport in cities including Shanghai, Beijing, Tianjin, and Shenyang. Photos from the 1980s show fleets of these two-seaters (which routinely squeezed in a lot more people) for hire as taxis in Shanghai, painted with uniform livery.

For hauling bigger loads, the Jiangxi Ganjiang Machinery Factory began manufacturing its 750 Z series, the country's first "large emission" motorized tricycle in 1969. The user manual featured a photo that would be familiar to rural-dwellers today: a boxy three-wheeler with an enclosed driver's cabin and spacious bed for transporting goods, driving past verdant rice paddies. After reforms in the 1980s made it legal for farmers to sell surplus crops grown on their land, both human-powered and motorized tricycles—including new, electrified models—became essential for transporting produce, as well as villagers, to the city.

Passenger-tricycles are still putt-putting their way around cities

Tricycles are often used to transport passengers, regardless of legality

Beng beng drivers' disregard of traffic laws is one reason behind the crackdowns

today, many serving as unlicensed taxis, rather literally named *beng beng* (蹦 蹦 , "jump jump") or *sanbengzi* (三 蹦 子 , "jump tricycle") due to the bumpiness of the ride. Similar to Southeast Asian tuk-tuks, *beng beng* are modified flat-bed tricycles with seats, a roof, side enclosures, and doors. They tend to congregate around train stations and suburban subway stops to serve commuters' "last mile," usually in areas without public transportation or during late-night hours after buses stop running.

The *beng beng* also has a lookalike cousin, the "old-age scooter," which isn't normally available for hire but instead transports aging urbanites to the produce market and the park, and their grandchildren to school.

Beng beng had their heyday in the first decade of the 2000s, when China's urban sprawl outpaced the development of both public transit and law enforcement in suburban neighborhoods—according to motorcycle news portal MTUO and the CAAM, motorized tricycle production increased around 20 percent a year from 2005 until 2015, when it began to decrease.

Today, though, many cities are cracking down on the vehicles, citing concerns such as the impossibility of licensing or insuring tricycles for passenger transport under current regulations, or the lack of training or vehicle registration required to own and drive one. In 2013, the government of Shijiazhuang, Hebei, claimed that tricycles caused over 30 traffic accidents in the city per day. The city prohibited both pedal and motorized trikes from driving inside its Second Ring Road and on major roads inside the Third Ring Road.

Yet even Shijiazhuang realized the futility of a total ban: Over the decades, tricycles had also become standard vehicles for water and gas delivery, couriers, the postal service, street sanitation, and other essential sectors. The government could only ask these public service tricycles to get new paint jobs and register with the city traffic control bureau, while promising closer inspections to make sure they don't run red lights, drive in motor vehicle lanes, or break other traffic laws.

Meanwhile, the crackdowns have invited dissent. A Ms. Sun told the People's Daily that Shijiazhuang's ban was going to raise expenses for small-business owners like herself, who would have to hire vans to transport goods rather than use their own tricycles "at virtually no cost." Ordinary citizens pointed out the convenience of *beng beng* in small streets where buses can't run, or neighborhoods without enough legal taxis. "The focus should be on making more traffic regulations for tricycles...rather than a simple 'all or nothing' approach," complained a Mr. Ma.

Then there are complaints from the drivers themselves, often rural-to-urban migrants attracted to the profession due to its flexibility and low barriers of entry. In 2014, *beng beng* drivers working the suburban Dalianpo, Guanzhuang, and Shuangqiao neighborhoods of Beijing reported monthly incomes of 4,000 to 7,000 RMB (average monthly income in Beijing was 6,463 RMB that year), and costs between 2,000 and 3,000 RMB to buy a secondhand tricycle ("a new one's not worth buying [since] it might get confiscated by police," one driver told the Beijing Youth Daily).

The same year, Beijing began a citywide crackdown on tricycles, including both *beng beng* and three-wheelers modified into food trucks or roadside stalls. Urban management (*chengguan*) officers were sent to 78 neighborhoods to confiscate unregistered vehicles and arrest drivers, with the eventual goal of banning diesel and electric tricycles inside the Sixth Ring Road.

In 2015, Li Fu, a driver in Fangshan district, injured three *chengguan* while resisting arrest, but got a comparatively light sentence of a year in prison after telling a sympathetic judge, "My mother is ill, my children are at school, and I drive a tricycle just to support my family." (Other drivers don't seem to be letting the still-ongoing raids affect business—"Take you somewhere on my way?" an enterprising driver near Beijing's Dalianpo station once shouted to journalists while sprinting for his vehicle, eager not to lose business even while escaping an anticipated police visit to the area.)

For the last two years, it seemed that bike-share apps might succeed where heavy-handed raids failed to finally drive tricycles off the road. Some *beng beng* drivers were reportedly vandalizing share-bikes parked on their turf. "The starting price for us used to be 10 RMB, but [with bikes], people can now travel for 50 cents to 1 RMB," one driver told Beijing's Morning Post.

Lately, though, the successive failures of bike apps like Coolqi, Xiaoming, Bluegogo, and, most alarmingly, ofo, have added another twist to the tale. As millions of defunct bikes get hauled out of Chinese cities to be trashed or recycled, usually on the back of large electric tricycles, the scrappy three-wheeler may be having the last laugh. - Hatty Liu

Originally published in March 2017

Last Stop

As ticket vendors disappear from China's buses, their legend remains

In the early 1960s, the Chinese people were asked to learn from Lei Feng. A semi-mythical foot-soldier assiduously devoted to Mao Zedong Thought and serving the people, Lei's legend helped the Communist Party to rally a nation still reeling from the disastrous Great Leap Forward.

In the 1990s, as China's new market economy picked up speed, the people were given a new ideological model: a Beijing public transit ticket vendor named Li Suli (李素丽).

Li's backstory, like Lei's, was emphatically ordinary. The daughter of a bus conductor, Li dreamed of becoming a newscaster, but scored 12 points too low on the entrance exams to go to college. She then joined Beijing Bus Route 60 and, believing that "even the least prestigious jobs need to be done well," became the best and hardest working ticket vendor she could be. In her slogan-filled, 18-year career, she purportedly became the "cane of the elderly," prepared newspapers and spare cushions for passengers, and once shamed a passenger by cleaning up his spit from the floor. While the rest of the the country was making demands about job security, social mobility, and increased wages under the new market economy, Li served years at a humble job with a responsible attitude and smile, eventually earning the title "Nation's Model Worker" for demonstrating that old Party adage, "To labor is the most glorious thing."

Ironically, 20 years after Li became the nation's exemplar of the ordinary, commonplace worker, her job has become all but obsolete. Across China, contact card systems and standardized fares have taken over vendors' basic role, while automated recordings and smartphones replaced their use at announcing stops and giving travel directions. Most Chinese cities have already done away with the position. In August, 2015, Shanghai announced that they would put "vendor-less buses" on all of their routes except four that departed from the train station, citing itself as one of the last cities in China to catch up with the times.

Today the last stand of this disappearing profession is Beijing, Li's home base. Even there, the system is slowly changing. In July 2016, ticket vendors on Beijing's Bus Route 300 went on strike to protest the phasing out of their position from the city's transit system.

Among their grievances, as told by a spokesperson who documented the incidents online, the ticket vendors were protesting the loss of their "iron rice bowl," the lifetime job security that used to be guaranteed by China's socialist economy. "Vendors work hard, have never done anything wrong, yet we've been told that our work will be replaced by machines and security guards," a vendor under the alias of Liu Ying

PHOTOGRAH BY VCG

Beijing is the last major city
in China to regularly employ
ticket collectors

reported. They also protested the fact that the transit company, which is part of a state-owned conglomerate, had not announced plans to place laid-off workers in other positions at the company. "We're getting up there in age and truly can't change our vocation," Liu complained.

Reactions from Beijingers who followed the incident online were mixed, with several pointing out that working hard at the same job for many years hardly qualified a person for job security *anywhere* in the current economy, never mind in a role that is now redundant. Up and down the country, iron rice bowls had been shattering since the 1980s. Ticket vendors, in the capital especially, had been insulated until now by the inertia of state enterprises and their bloated benefit networks.

Whereas ticket vendors once represented values of old-fashioned hard work and honest reward vital to a newly reformed society, they now symbolize inefficiency and outdated attitudes about employment, which have no place in an increasingly technocratic and competitive economy. Primarily older women (and some older men) who've worked long years in their company at the detriment of gaining other skills, ticket vendors fall under what economists call the "overemployment" phenomenon in "reforming socialist economies"; their grievances and occasional protests remain a delicate subject in China as it struggles to balance economic growth and social harmony.

Both Beijing and Shanghai's transit authorities have refused our request for comment. The original copies of the Sina Weibo posts by the spokesperson covering the strike have been removed, though the account remains active.

Aside from machines, the other nemesis of the ticket vendors is the transit security guard. This is a relatively new position, also mostly found in Beijing and Shanghai; it was added to Beijing buses in 2016 as vendors were laid off. The two groups are polar opposites in a number of ways. Ticket vendors are affectionately called "ticket vending aunties." They are required to have a Beijing household registration and collect generous benefits despite below-average pay, around 4,300 RMB as reported online.

The guards are often young, in their teens and early 20s. They are also reported to be migrants from outside of Beijing, and are stereotyped as apathetic, ignorant of local geography, and socially awkward in contrast to the poised and opinionated "aunties." Local media and online job posts also indicate that transit companies are trying to recruit guards and "service personnel" with college or technical school education in order to modernize their image. Guards are employed by private contractors, whose job ads indicate that they are paid only half the reported average salary of ticket vendors and mention no social insurance.

Though divided about the utility of ticket vendors, Beijingers more or less prefer them to the guards, or "safety personnel" as they are official known. This mostly arises from the general animosity that Beijing natives have for *waidiren* (外地人), non-locals who, as the old story goes, are invading their city and taking their jobs. Liu's comments specified that it was "Beijing" vendors who were protesting machines and "non-local" guards. The strikers' Weibo spokesperson also argued that having local Beijingers on Beijing buses presented "Beijing characteristics" (北京特色), rare things to find in this day and age.

However, this incident, arising from the ticket vendors' precarious economic value, has also highlighted how symbolically the profession is as robust and resilient as it was in the days of Li

Suli. A couple of bloggers sympathetic to the ticket vendors' cause have referenced the 1950s propaganda film *Spring Reigns Everywhere* (《春满人间》) and 1990s film *Shanghai Fever* (《股疯》), both of which feature ticket-vending characters who embody different nostalgic ideas about the profession. *Spring*'s Zhu Xiuyun greets her passengers sweetly and efficiently climbs down to help a child aboard. *Shanghai Fever*'s Fan Li likes to shout at errant cyclists, but to her passengers she is straight-talking, wryly humorous, and surprisingly kind—like a mother hen, she fusses, but it's all for the protection of her young.

The legacy of Li Suli, as well as the depiction of ticket vendors in these films, lives on. Beijingers who commented in support of the striking vendors were nostalgic (and slightly tongue-in-cheek) about hearing their "auntie's" brassy voice and her ceaseless admonitions of what you should and shouldn't be doing. After all, being told when to let the elderly sit, shouted at to keep order, and scrutinized for every action by the well-meaning voice of authority is as quintessential a Chinese characteristic as any. It's entangled in the millennia of history of social hierarchy, in which authority figures had a moral obligation to guide, mold, and correct, whether or not it was any of their business.

It's also reflective of people's continued anxieties about order and safety while living in a large population and changing times. Shanghai's four bus routes from the train station are actually required by city laws to retain their ticket vendors; Beijing transit authorities also say that double-decker buses will continue to employ vendors. These are considered particularly challenging routes, as the migrant population from the train station are believed to need extra supervision and street directions, and everyone needs reminders to move their luggage. The narrow stairs and isolated upper deck of double-deckers are just asking for accidents, thefts, and ticket dodgers.

Reminiscences from former ticket vendors have appeared in Chinese media in recent years. They paint a rather clearer-eyed picture of what was ultimately a low-status job, when stripped of ideology. Two men in their 80s, who started working as ticket vendors in the 1940s, vividly told The Hangzhou Evening News of being hours on their feet, pressed against sweaty bodies of passengers all summer long, mistaken for beggars collecting alms, beaten up by ticket dodgers, and even shot at during the Chinese Civil War. A soon-to-be laid off vendor in Zhunnan, Anhui, told the local paper that she hates it when passengers address her rudely, but likes it when the children call her "auntie." She also described missing lunch breaks, which were only 20 minutes long, whenever traffic puts her behind schedule. Meanwhile, a former vendor from Nanchang wrote of vendors having practically no holidays and having their breaks times used up by the company's safety checks, political education, and team-building events.

And what was the fate of Li Suli, whose story taught countless Chinese the gloriousness of working for the nation regardless of prestige, security, or pay? She's still officially employed by the transit system in Beijing at the time of writing, but she has not been a ticket vendor since 1998. Instead, shortly after starring in the Party's 1996 "Learn From Li Suli" campaign, she started a transit information hotline, where she supposedly advises callers on both transit and personal matters to this day. - Hatty Liu

Originally published in November 2016

Flight Risk

Despite surging passenger numbers, airlines in China are struggling with delays, pilot shortages, and declining profits

The airline's name was Lucky Air, but at least one passenger didn't find this auspicious enough. In October 2017, a 76-year-old woman boarding a flight in Anqing, Anhui province, decided to toss some coins into the jet's engine in a misguided effort to ensure good fortune.

The plane was grounded for safety reasons, and passengers had to wait until the next morning for a rescheduled flight. It wasn't the first time this type of behavior has occurred: Another pensioner in Shanghai threw coins into an engine in June, leading to further delays for passengers.

The incident was a literal demonstration of the multitudes of problems that can ground China's flights—even the toss of a coin. As the industry strains under the weight of its own growth, profits and departure times are getting ever more fickle.

Shortages of pilots and airspace loom, and reform is desperately needed, as even the mightiest players in the sector struggle with an increasingly difficult business environment.

Take China Southern, Asia's largest airline, which recorded over 60 billion RMB in revenue in the first half of 2017, an 11 percent increase over the same period the previous year. Yet the airline's profitability has decreased, thanks to growing operational costs like jet fuel. The airline still made 2.77 billion RMB in the first half, but that was down 11 percent from 2016.

And China Southern is one of the lucky ones. Hong Kong carrier Cathay Pacific is still coming to terms with the billion RMB loss it posted for the first half of 2017, in what its own analysts, cited in the South China Morning Post in October, dubbed the airline's "worst operating results in history." It came after Cathay had posted a loss of half a billion RMB in 2016.

Cathay is attempting to slash salaries in order to cope (after already shedding 600 staff), but there are already obvious signs of why this measure is a risky one.

It's difficult to quantify the size of the pilot shortage in China, given the rapid changes in the industry, but analysts have indicated that, on current projections, China will need 5,000 new pilots every year for the next 20 years, and it's uncertain whether global supply will be able to keep up with that demand.

So when Cathay Pacific's attempts to cut salaries became known, recruitment company Longreach Aviation organized a roadshow event in what was a overt attempt to poach Cathay Pacific's undoubtedly disgruntled pilots on behalf of mainland airlines. (The roadshow event, planned for October, was abruptly shut down, with the recruiters blaming "legal issues.")

The pilot shortage has its upsides, for pilots at least. Pilot Zhang Lin (pseudonym) says that flying had become a popular career

4

✈ 국제선출수
國際線登机
國際線登乘
International
Boarding

epartures 4

A person who interfere
screening process or attach
shall be fined no more

choice, and "one aspect is definitely the high salary."

"A huge part of that salary comes from experience," he explains. "A captain will earn more than a co-pilot. Salaries across the various airlines are different. Big airlines in China are not the best in the business, in terms of salaries."

A quick web search reveals multitudes of vacancies. There's an A320 captain position in Hangzhou, being offered 25,833 USD per month, after tax, with 45 days of paid leave. A first officer is wanted in Tianjin for B747s, for 11,200 USD per month, but with increasing annual bonuses over the term of the three-year contract.

"The main reason [for the pilot shortage] is the rapid development of the industry in recent years," says Zhang. "After graduation, it takes a pilot five to eight years to become a productive asset. The airlines simply don't have enough pilots in reserve," he says. "We often hear cases of foreign pilots being recruited as well."

There are certainly perks for foreign pilots working in China. CNN cited one American pilot in 2016, Jeff Graham, who had been working 80 to 100-hour months in the US. After switching to a job based in Shenzhen, he worked 50-hour months for triple the salary.

But even as the number of commercial pilots grows, the airspace they are occupying remains startlingly small. The majority of China's airspace is controlled by the military due to the defense-oriented aviation system devised in the 1950s.

A 2012 paper in the journal of transportation technologies, written by academics from Northwestern Polytechnical University in Xi'an, China's aviation industry capital, makes clear the division between scholars who advocate for a closed-off military-controlled airspace system, and those pushing for a more open one.

This debate has long been at the core of aviation reform. "From the perspective of the use of airspace, its specific characteristics are reflected as that the need for military aviation comes first and the need for civil aviation comes second," the academics wrote, adding that this is the concept of "absolute security."

Those pushing for openness still need to acknowledge the importance of the security aspect, but contend that "absolute security" is unrealistic. The paper characterizes this side of the debate as arguing that "the concept of 'absolute security' for airspace legislation has caused uneconomic results such as serious waste of airspace resources, and low utilization of airspace, and it is bound to hinder China's civil air transport industry."

The friction between these camps persists today, etched out in state maps of China's airspace. As pilot and former China correspondent James Fallows points out in his book *China Airborne*, maps of Chinese airspace are considered too sensitive for foreign eyes. "But if you could look, you'd see at once that the areas not controlled by the military are relatively thin, crabbed corridors connecting the biggest cities," he wrote. "All the rest has been off limits to everyone except the People's Liberation Army."

The lack of civilian airspace is partly why the seven worst airports in the world for delays are all in China. Not only are civilian flights kept on narrow corridors, which limits their options in the event they need to change course, but there are also frequent instances of passengers being told that their flights have been canceled due to "military exercises."

The space available for civilian flights has increased, but civilians aren't privy to knowing how much bigger it's gotten.

"The growth in flight density has been greater than the growth in airspace," Zhang said. "But I've observed over the course of my career and in recent years, both the route density and airspace have increased."

There have also been openly announced efforts to remedy the issues associated with this shortage of airspace, even if the airspace details themselves remain secret. In May 2017, Cai Jun, deputy director of the Air Traffic Control commission (which is administered by both the State Council and Central Military Commission), told media that a series of proposals were being submitted to deal with the problem by integrating civilian and military airspace bodies. "We understand that reforming the management of the airspace...is an essential need," Reuters quoted him as saying. "Pushing ahead with civil and military integration is an important measure and a requirement that will help us adjust to the global air traffic management system and accelerate China's transformation into an aviation power."

Fallows points out that the successful integration of these civilian and military networks will be a challenging task because it can't just be achieved through brute willpower—and that the stakes go beyond the aviation sector. "Success in this realm really does require the integration of a wide variety of 'hard' and 'soft' skills and technologies, and both public and private resources," he says. The pilot shortage and integration of military and civilian airspace, according to Fallows, are a microcosm of broader issues China has to contend with as it develops into an advanced economy.

Fallows points out parallels with the evolution of American airspace controls: "By the end of World War II, the US military exercised control over an enormous amount of airspace over

America, a natural legacy of broader wartime controls of the economy. From the military's point of view, it would have been 'safer' and more convenient to leave all those controls in place. But the federal government arranged a gradual and substantial shift of airspace from military to civilian and commercial use; otherwise, the airline and general-aviation markets would never fully have developed."

"The next big test for China's aerospace ambitions is how the government will handle this choice between maximum 'security' and greater opportunities for an important new business to grow," he says.

Fallows makes the life-or-death stakes of these reforms clear through an incident outlined in *China Airborne*. While flying as a co-pilot on a tiny four-seat plane traveling between Changsha and Zhuhai in 2006, he encountered mountains that were higher than the altitude they had been assigned by flight control. Thus, they needed to radio for permission to climb higher. "On the GPS-based moving map in the cockpit, we saw the ridge draw closer. We couldn't legally turn around, since that would be deviating from our clearance. Nor—again, without breaking rules—could we decide to climb on our own," he wrote.

"If we kept on straight and level, within ten minutes we'd crash. Then eight. Then six." Declaring an emergency and turning away was one option, but it would have severe repercussions, particularly because, as it turned out, they were being tailed by a military jet.

Despite repeated radio requests, they were greeted with silence. It took a Japan Airlines pilot, who had been eavesdropping, to intercede on their behalf to get the attention of air traffic controllers, who then granted them permission. Fallows never found a reason for the delay, but suspected that the flight controllers simply hadn't dealt with private pilots before, so they didn't know what to do.

In the decade since that incident, the situation has improved dramatically, but delays are still mounting at Chinese airports. In the first six months of 2017, the proportion of flights arriving on time was 71 percent, 6 percentage points lower than the same period in 2016, the South China Morning Post reported. In June 2017 alone, barely half the flight were on time.

A quarter of the hazards were reported to be caused by "military activity," while the biggest proportion were caused by weather. Zhang points out that within China's large landmass, there are vast differences in landscape and significant potential for weather delays. Another headache has been fairly recently added to the woes of flight controllers; 800 flights were delayed in the first half of 2017 due to drones flying too close to airports.

There is also the threat of "black flights" by unregistered aircraft. In 2014, Wang Xia, secretary-general of the China General Aviation Committee, told state media that about 60 percent of more than 3,300 general aviation aircraft in China were unregistered, partly due to the disorganized nature of the registration process. These flights can pose a severe hazard to flight safety and also cause delays, though few garner media attention. An incident in 2010 involved a black flight leaving the city of Jiaxing, Zhejiang province. The plane was classed as a UFO and caused multiple flights out of the nearby Shanghai Pudong Airport to be delayed.

And then, there are the delays caused by passengers. Due to ongoing media reports of unruly mobs (and coin-tossing grannies) at Chinese airports, Chinese travelers have developed an unfortunate reputation of being troublesome. This is perhaps unfair, given the massive numbers of travelers and relatively small numbers of incidents, but the incidents do hint at deeper problems. There have been constant reports of passengers attempting to open emergency doors during flights, abuse of flight attendants, fist-fights between angry passengers, and demands for compensation for a variety of inconveniences, as passengers take to the sky in ever greater numbers for the first time.

Meanwhile, China's ultra-rich look unlikely to take flights on the main airlines as the private jet industry gets off the ground. In October 2017, China Daily cited Thomas Flohr, founder of private jet company Vistajet, as saying that 17 percent of their customers now come from China and that the proportion is growing. "Private jet business on the Chinese mainland is still relatively new, and it is our great focus within the Asia-Pacific region," he said, adding that the minimum net worth of the company's customers is around 200 million USD, and they tend to be between their late 20s and 50s.

Zhang believes that growth in private flights is likely to be one of the biggest changes in the industry in the coming years. "There are still many factors affecting the development of this industry, such as purchasing, operation and maintenance, airspace and the state of airport openness, difficulty requesting and getting approval for flight plans, and so on," he said. "But the number of business jet flights has been growing steadily, and aircraft manufacturers are eyeing China as a growing market."

It would seem that while China's aviation sector has well and truly taken off, where it heads next is still up in the air. - David Dawson

Originally published in November 2017

Chapter Five:
Entertainment

"For nothing was there except my mat and pillow—
Gone was the world of mists and clouds.
And so with the pleasures of this life;
All pass, as water flows eastward."

- Li Bai, "A Visit to Skymother Mountain in a Dream"

East Side Story

After a 'Miserables' beginning, can Chinese
musicals finally make rent?

When tickets for the musical *Letters* sold out within a minute of going online, no one was more surprised than its lead actor Zheng Yunlong, who had promoted the show on his Weibo account only to learn he was already too late.

It was the moment for which "I have been waiting for 10 years," Zheng commented beneath his own post. Though recognized as one of China's top musical performers, having won best actor at the 2018 Musical Academy Awards in Beijing, Zheng is probably used to seeing empty seats in the theater: He once played a show in Harbin to an audience of 10.

Back in 2017, as Chinese cinema took in nearly 60 billion RMB, musicals made just 217 million RMB. Shanghai, the largest market in the country, only has about 30,000 to 40,000 regular theatergoers out of a population of more than 240 million, as industry watcher Wei Jiayi told news site Jiemian.

After six years laboring in musical obscurity, Zheng's own career took off when he appeared in the TV talent show *Super Vocal*, alongside 35 other professional musical and opera singers, telling viewers he signed up in hopes that "more people will learn about musicals, and be more willing to see a musical in the theater." With a rating of 9.5 out of 10 on review site Douban, *Super Vocal* became one of the most successful variety shows of 2018 with Zheng, a finalist, as one of its biggest winners: His Weibo following increased from 2,000 to 830,000 at the time of writing.

Though this burgeoning "idol culture" in musical theater is controversial—an irate reviewer on Douban opines that audiences drawn by the TV stars are not true musical fans—the boost to Zheng's profile was undeniable. Since appearing on the show, Zheng has starred in two musicals; all of his 18 total performances have rapidly sold out, and his new fans seem likely to stick around.

"Going to the theater is addictive," an audience member surnamed Guo says after a production of Zheng's *Murder Ballad* in Beijing in March. A recent convert to musicals, Guo said she already had tickets to see *Cats* and *Romeo and Juliet* later this year.

Compared to the first quarter of the previous year, ticket-selling platform Damai has reported a 28.6 percent increase in sales and six times the amount of revenue for a total of 517 musical performances in 2019, which include touring Western imports, localized translations, and—currently the least popular—Chinese originals.

The first Western musical performed in China was *Les Misérables*, which had 21 performances in its original language in Shanghai in 2002. Productions of *Cats*, *The Sound of Music*, and *The Phantom*

Scene from *Butterflies*

of the Opera at the Shanghai Grand Theater followed. According to entertainment site D-entertainment, in 2015, 64.2 percent of the whole musical box office income went to imports.

The market for translated musicals has also been growing, as represented by a localized version of *Mamma Mia* in 2011 (which had Donna singing about going gambling in Macau, instead of Las Vegas or Monaco). Zheng's most popular roles have been in Chinese versions of Broadway hits like *Jekyll and Hyde* and *Man of La Mancha*.

By comparison, there was only one original Chinese work in the top 10 musicals at China's box office in 2017, a production of comedy troupe Kaixin Mahua called *Men*. When fans do talk about Chinese musicals, they are still discussing *Butterflies*, an adaptation of the folk tale "The Butterfly Lovers." First produced 12 years ago, it won the Judge's Choice Award at the Daegu International Musical Festival in 2008—the first time a Chinese musical won an international award.

Butterflies's producer, Li Dun, is displeased by this state of affairs. "About three years ago, I predicted that China's musical market would see a boom. But I didn't expect everyone would be doing imported works and translations," Li laments. "They think it's easier than doing originals. But the fact is none of them are making money. The royalties are too high."

By contrast, Li, known as the "godfather of the Chinese original musical," has been concentrating on indigenous productions for over 30 years. In 1997, he produced *White Snake*, based on another classic folk tale, with famous musician San Bao. Regarded as the first Chinese musical, the play had 1,200 performances in Shenzhen.

Li's other works also tell Chinese stories. In *Love U, Teresa*, the

Li (center) and his team discussing the creation of *Ah, Kuliang*

spirit of the late singer Teresa Teng helps a young musician follow his dreams; *Ah, Kuliang* is about an American son of missionaries who grew up in China and tries to return to the country after the Cold War; *Papa, I Only Sing for You* follows the relationship between a pop star and her foster father; *Mama, Love Me Once Again* tells about the bond and conflicts between a single mother and her son out of wedlock. "We have such a long history and such rich cultural resources. There are so many stories we can tell," says Li.

However, says Li, attempts to make musicals "embody Eastern aesthetics" have been fraught. He recalls composer San Bao and Canadian director Gilles Maheau quarreling on the set of *Butterflies*. "The Westerners thought it was unbelievable that people became butterflies after death, while this plot device is well-accepted in China," Li explains.

Audiences were similarly conflicted: During one show in Shanghai, a viewer took exception to the storyline and screamed, "You liars! This is not our 'Butterfly Lovers!'"

Now, however, many ask Li when the show will be revived. "Maybe we did it too early," says Li. "The audience need to be guided [to appreciate musicals]. It will be a long process, but someone has to do it anyway."

Most Chinese theatergoers buy tickets based on reputation, so every year "only the five most famous plays can get attention," Wei, who is the chief editor of WeChat-based theater news outlet Haoxi, told Jiemian. This means Broadway and West End works, whether original or in translation, have the advantage.

However, Li insists original Chinese works are better because the translations are often bad in quality. "Sometimes, I feel the actors get depressed singing these poorly translated songs," he muses.

Getting investment for domestic productions is a different matter, though: In 2019, an industry insider indentified as "Xiao Si" told Jiemian that the production cost of an original musical is usually 10 times that of a common stage drama, but the return is highly uncertain. Most theater companies rely on state support, which requires adhering to staid narratives and politically correct values.

The China National Art Fund sponsors 10 original musicals annually for a maximum 4 million RMB each, but "most of the money went to stated-owned companies," Li notes. "And what plays are they performing? Just some empty, grandiose stories." It's not rare to see lots of money sunk into bad productions, he explains.

Lack of talent is another problem. Veteran musical actors are in short supply, thanks to the relatively brief history of the format, while younger actors lack skills. "The standard China's theatre academies set for their students is too low," San Bao told China Literature and Art Criticism magazine. "Musical theater students need musicianship, acting talent, and body coordination, but few students currently have all three."

According to the Shanghai Conservatory Music, the number of students auditioning for its musical theater program increased by 46 percent this year. However, Li says few stay in the profession long, estimating that about 80 percent of musical performers end up changing their career—many lured by the higher pay of pop singing or film acting.

From the audience, there are also accusations of price-gouging. Seats for Zheng's *Murder Ballad* cost 380 to 880 RMB in Beijing, but at its previous stop in Shanghai, the most expensive seat was only 280 RMB. "That's the reality of our market; some people just can't do things the right way," Li alleges. "Sometimes, I feel like I am making musicals in hell." (Zheng himself had obliquely criticized the unreasonable high price of his show on Weibo).

But Li isn't giving up: He is still trying to stage a new original musical, *Shen Nan Blvd*—while coping with a last-minute loss of investors, another symptom of the immature market. "This is simply a test from heaven...the show will go on," Li vows. "So long as people enter the theater, I'm confident I can make them stay."
- Sun Jiahui (孙佳慧)

Originally published in May 2019

Funny Business

Can China's comedy scene finally stand up?

Thirty minutes before showtime, a young Chinese crowd is already thronging the entrance of Shanghai's Comedy UN, recently relocated to an office building near Nanjing Road that still smells of fresh paint. Inside, dance music pulsates through the small, dark theater as 32-year-old comedian-owner Storm Xu fidgets, preparing for the night's performance.

Xu is no stand-up newbie, having quit his day job at General Motors in 2015 to found Comedy UN. "I didn't want to keep performing in sh-tty rooms," he explains. "For comedy performances in China, a lot of owners of cafes and bars will let you use their space. But they actually couldn't care less about comedy; all they want to do is increase foot traffic."

His club, which holds 130 folding chairs, now organizes up to six performances each week with a roster of 20 Mandarin and 15 English-speaking comedians. "I feel fulfilled being able to nurture other talents and give them a venue for their comedy," he explains, noting that comedy venues in Mandarin were non-existent when he returned to his native Shanghai in 2012, after studying in Australia. Back then, Xu had exclusively performed at English-language open mic nights, regaling expat audiences with gripes about his ex-girlfriend.

Now, he performs entire Mandarin stand-up shows for the Chinese military—a sure sign of the rising popularity of this imported comedy form in China. One major reason is the plethora of new platforms, which allow comedians to create and promote their own content, from short-video apps like Douyin and Kuaishou to self-produced web shows and podcasts.

According to Beijing-based comic Daniel Dan, this model is unprecedented in China's entertainment industry. "The idea of a 'grassroots artist' is a relatively new concept. [Traditional entertainers] had to study at a drama institute or underneath a master. Very rarely were talents 'discovered' like in the West," he notes, discussing his own uncommon beginnings as a biochemistry-turned-English major at the Beijing Institute of Technology. "But in modern stand-up, you can make your own career."

According to David Moser, the former dean of Peking University's Yenching Academy and a scholar of Chinese humor, a master-apprentice lineage was essential of China's traditional *xiangsheng* ("crosstalk") comedy prior to 1949. But even after the founding of the PRC, a rigid model persisted as *danwei*, or state-operated work units, hired performers to learn Beijing-dialect *xiangsheng* and sent them to perform around the country. "Comedy became highly politicized because it was viewed as a mechanism to help standardize spoken Chinese," Moser explains.

Storm Xu performs at his club Comedy UN

A Comedy Club China comic performs in Xiamen

Comedy first saw a revolution in the 1980s through television—namely CCTV's annual Spring Festival Gala. Its inaugural broadcast in 1983 featured *xiangsheng* comedians as hosts, and skits which satirized everyday conditions, albeit avoiding overtly political topics. "China was in the process of urbanizing, and a lot of skits featured country bumpkins moving to the city and essentially getting everything wrong in the process," says Moser. "It resonated with what real people were going through."

Eva Hart, an amateur stand-up who grew up in Jilin province, agrees. "I remember when I was a girl, every punchline of every joke from the Gala inevitably became phrases of the year." One of her favorite skits, from 2001, featured northern comic Zhao Benshan tricking a healthy man into exchanging his bicycle for old crutches.

"Now, most people just watch it to make fun of it," Hart notes with a trace of sadness. Indeed, today's audiences have found the Gala's attempts to address modern topics to be toothless at best, and offensive at worst (a 2018 skit in blackface, "celebrating" Sino-African relations, comes to mind). While Hart chalks up the Gala's decline to more sophisticated audience tastes and media competition, others blame censors' over-cautiousness about satirizing socio-economic schisms.

The comedy revolution continued with the commercialization of Chinese television during the 1990s. "When CCTV started selling television advertising, it meant that the 'free money' to produce whatever sort of comedy show you wanted was gone," says Moser. "To survive, comedy had to become more market-savvy, and began to look for inspiration from modern life, as well as from the West." This not only led to a decline in *xiangsheng*'s visibility, but also the rise of sitcoms, from 1993's *I Love My Family* to 2009's *Love*

Apartment (inevitably, inspiration often led to imitation: the latter was accused of cribbing whole plots and jokes from American standards like *Friends* and *How I Met Your Mother*).

Stand-up was conspicuously missing from this line-up. Bilingual comic Jesse Appell, the Boston-born founder of Beijing's US-China Comedy Center, thinks that the language itself was a challenge: "Mandarin has no linguistic, cultural, or historical equivalent to stand-up comedy," he declares. "Anything that's funny that is not traditional *xiangsheng* is simply referred to as 'talk show' (脱口秀, *tuokouxiu*). Even a podcast can be a 'talk show' if it's funny."

Things began to change, though, in 2010, when Chinese-American comic Huang Xi, better known in English by his stage name, Joe Wong, performed at the annual Radio and Television Correspondents' Association Gala in Washington D.C. Videos of Wong's act went viral in the mainland due to the way he poked gentle fun at then-US Vice President Joe Biden, who was in attendance. The Jilin native's mockery of his own career path—he'd obtained a PhD in biochemistry from Rice University, before pursuing comedy—also resonated with mainland comics.

In 2013, Wong returned to China to host a CCTV show—a big morale boost for the local Beijing comedy scene. The following year, Canadian comic Mark Rowswell, or Dashan, known as China's "most famous foreigner" for his performances of *xiangsheng* on state TV in the early 90s, returned "on a mission to introduce Western stand-up to China...working the [national] university circuit on his own dime," according to The Atlantic.

Tony Chou of Jinan, Shandong province, was one of the new generation of comics drawn to stand-up by videos of Wong. Like Comedy UN owner Xu, Chou began attending English-language open mic nights in 2013, and recalls the difficulties many of his peers had with the format. "In the early days, you would see a lot of Chinese comedians going up on stage with scripts or flashcards in their hands, or frantically trying to memorize their jokes in front of the mirror before the show," Chou laughs. "They didn't understand improvisation, and viewed stand-up comedy as funny drama."

In 2014, visiting Irish comedian Des Bishop asked Chou to help him start a comedy club, Youmo Xiaoqu (幽默小区, Humor Section), which put on Chinese shows roughly once a month. Chou picked up the slack once Bishop left China, quitting his reporter job at CCTV and establishing a long-running partnership with The Bookworm, a popular Beijing bookstore where Youmo Xiaoqu now hosts a weekly show. Having recently celebrated the club's five-year anniversary, Chou boasts that the club is profitable even without a permanent venue, with a pool of 60 Beijing-based comedians and 100 others across China.

Even so, Chou has supplemented his income with a day job as a producer, writer, and performer for internet portal Sohu; corporate gigs; and Chinese shows on the Norwegian Cruise Line. He also appeared in a Hong Kong film. "At the moment, the only way a Chinese person can do stand-up full-time is if they take another job in the industry: running shows; finding television or hosting jobs, or managing and owning their own club," notes David Jacobs, the manager of Beijing's English-language Comedy Club China.

One challenge of live performances in China is that increased profitability can come at the risk of government involvement: "Open mic nights and shows can't get too big, or else it might make the government uneasy and they may put restrictions on crowds," Daniel Dan notes. "But how can you make real money with small crowds?"

Xu claims that the risk of operating Comedy UN is "not worth losing any sleep over." When crackdowns come, however, they can be sudden and sometimes permanent. Comedy Club China lost its former venue at a café in Beijing's Wudaokou quarter after an audience member complained about a joke on a social issue. "Our open mic nights are kind of in a gray space. Besides, large gatherings of foreigners attract government attention, especially if they are giving unscripted speeches," manager Jacobs explains.

Jacobs cites the sudden closure of Shanghai's Kung Fu Komedy club, shortly before the China International Import Summit in October 2018, as a cautionary tale. Previously credited with making Shanghai China's "comedy capital," the influential club's shuttering sent shockwaves across the scene, though former co-owner Andy Curtain has stated it was "less dramatic than it sounds" when authorities came to the club during a Wednesday open mic night: "They were like, 'Yeah, you're not allowed to do this anymore,'" he told the *Lost in America* podcast. There were options to re-open, but after consideration, Curtain decided it was like "putting a Band-Aid on a sinking ship."

Live comedy is not the only medium that has had to deal with sudden regulatory reversals: In July 2018, Youku's localized version of *Saturday Night Live* was taken down without explanation soon after release (then returned quietly, even renewing for a second season). Also in 2018, Neihan Duanzi, ByteDance's popular app for memes and humorous videos, was abruptly shut down for "vulgar content," much to the disappointment of its 30 million users. One anonymous user lamented: "When Duanzi was censored, I felt a certain pain in my heart, like someone had taken my child from me."

"Humor doesn't have to be political to be funny," Moser asserts. "Older comedians who have already developed their craft seldom complain. However, the younger generations, who are trying to create something new, feel [the government influence] much more strongly."

Tony Chou knows this all too well: In 2017, he was employed by Sohu to perform on the popular late-night internet talk show, the *Liang Huan Show*. Despite quickly gaining popularity, only nine of the 12 episodes of the season were broadcast; five can still be found on the internet. Reportedly, the show fell on the wrong side of the authorities due to a single joke. "As comics, we all understand that we need to be within the boundaries of some line," Tony Chou comments. "The problem is that the line is always changing."

Some comics have dealt with this by self-censoring. The Chinese system often leads the country's comics to overly rely on self-deprecation, according to Hart. "In China, you can focus your jokes on your own individuality, but not individuality in the context of society." Many of Hart's jokes revolve around her American husband, and few Chinese comics develop ideas beyond family drama, dating issues, or job pressures.

That doesn't mean that Chinese comedy is devoid of diversity: Dan, who claims to have the "self-awareness" to stay away from political topics, often delves into his experiences growing up in a small Hunan village as a member of the Yao ethnic minority. One joke relates to the village custom of putting a 5 *kuai* bill in a dead person's open coffin, which led confused non-locals at the funeral to try to "one-up" one other by throwing in larger and larger denominations.

TV comedy contest *Xiao'ao Jianghu*

Hart believes that comedy remains empowering, in spite of these challenges. Comparing it to China's traditional *xiangsheng*, which is scripted and takes a long time to master, she notes that "stand-up is based on your own story; your own perspective. Everyone can participate because no one is the same. Everyone has a unique voice and perspective that are theirs alone."

For Dan, this was what drew him to comedy in the first place, after shows like *Friends* and *Shameless* helped him deal with depression during university. "When I first went to a comedy open-mic night...it was less about comedy and more like therapy," Dan recalls. "I hated studying biochemistry and I was in the process of coming out. I remember I started my set with a self-introduction, 'My name is Daniel Dan. I am gay.' Then my dad died and I turned to comedy to cope. For a while, I would start my set with, 'My name is Daniel Dan. My dad just died.'"

1. Eva Hart performs stand-up

2. Tony Chou celebrates the five-year anniversary of Youmo Xiaoqu

3. Comics perform at a Beijing open-mic night

4. Comedy Club China occasionally tours across the country

5. Comedy shows frequently sell out

The days of independent comics and unique perspectives may be numbered, however, as "comedy start-ups" flood the scene with venture capital. Sensing the advantages to monopolizing young talent, companies like Fun Factory (Xiao Guo Culture Company), Dan Li Ren, and Beijing Talk Show Club are hiring stand-up performers under exclusive contracts, funneling them into affiliated web shows or offline clubs and tours—and in the process, creating a model strikingly similar to the master-apprentice relationships of the past.

Beijing-based Dan Li Ren is funded by Tudou, the Alibaba-backed streaming site on which their contracted comics perform. In 2017, Shanghai's Fun Factory purchased the Chinese rights to *Comedy Central Roast*, a program in which comedians poke fun at a celebrity, after securing 120 million RMB from China Media Capital and Wang Sicong, scion of the Wanda Group.

Within a year, Fun Factory's localized version, *Roast*, had racked up over 3.6 billion views on streaming platform Tencent Video. "Everyone wanted to do stand-up after that," Dan explains. "But the TV show producers were from a different era; they didn't have a clue how to incorporate Western-style comedy into their programs." TV and web shows became increasingly varied, more comics were needed to fill the slots, but China's underdeveloped stand-up scene proved problematic. "Stand-up was underground and there was only a limited number of truly talented and experienced comedians," says Dan.

The competition within this small pool was cutthroat—often to the detriment of local comedy scenes. One independent comedian commented anonymously that Shenzhen was one of the hardest-hit scenes, as comics relocated to Shanghai with their Fun Factory contracts. Many are lured by the prospect that, if their offline performances under the company get laughs, they'll have a direct pipeline to be cast in Fun Factory or its investors' online programs.

More established comics are concerned by the effect these companies may have on the nascent stand-up scene, noting that the terms of the contract can be exploitative and monthly salaries are low, especially for young talents. The anonymous comedian compared the business model unfavorably to that of China's shared-bike industry, namely in the fierce competition to accrue talent and debt just to gain market share. "Their incentive is not to create the best comedy, but to grow their own teams."

"Creativity is not just about investing money and getting a return; the equation is much more complicated than that," notes Tony Chou. While he is excited about the new capital flooding into the comedy sphere, he worries that market influences could cause stand-up to follow the "K-pop model...[of] putting less emphasis on the individual and just finding good-looking people to tell jokes that other people write for them."

In spite of these concerns, Daniel Dan is currently signed to a start-up (which he declined to name), and is grateful to be allowed to make a living from his craft. His day job requires writing and directing Mandarin-language sketch comedy for other contracted comics at the company's clubs in Beijing, leaving his evenings free for his passion—English-language stand-up. "Jokes cannot be written in an office somewhere. The industry requires offline performances for the audience to determine if your ideas and jokes are actually funny," observes Dan, who explains that he hopes to "explain China to the world" through his comedy.

Tony Chou, though, is still doubtful of the new model's sustainability, noting that many web shows—the holy grail for comics, as well as investors—last only a couple of seasons. His work with Sohu has opened Chou's eyes to the unforeseen considerations of profit-making in programs, which often rely on one major underwriting sponsor because "most platforms assume people won't pay for content."

"In the West, there is one major stakeholder—the audience," reflects Chou, who is set to star in a forthcoming Sohu program modeled after Conan O'Brien's eponymous show. "In the Chinese model, you must worry about the audience, the sponsor, as well as the government. Producing something that all three can agree on is a nearly impossible task."

Still, Chou remains optimistic, noting that lower-tier cities are developing their own scenes. Independent clubs are popping up in cities like Shenyang, Xi'an, Qingdao, Xiamen, Taiyuan, Shijiazhuang, Chengdu, and Suzhou, though the best local talent still risk getting "poached" by comedy start-ups in Shanghai or Beijing.

"Stand-up comedy is on the rise and we must protect it," Chou notes with hope. "If we follow the early days of rock-and-roll in China—if we *don't* make waves, we will definitely succeed." - Emily Conrad

Originally published in May 2019

unenviable reputation of being coarse and exploitative, an image that its CEO, Su Hua, takes issue with. "In most cases the videos are simple depictions of joyful moments in everyday situations," Su told the Chinese site TechNode in 2016.

Kuaishou's fanbase is the 674 million-strong, lower-middle and working classes from parts of the country rarely depicted on mainstream TV or cinema screens—rural, undeveloped, mostly impoverished. They are the people who deliver your takeouts, serve your meals, manicure your nails and put together your iPhones. And what they sometimes lack in means or sophistication, they often make up for in enthusiasm, humor, innovation, and authenticity.

To many of them, Kuaishou is a celebration of "real China," as well as a rare, sometimes lucrative opportunity to grab some limelight. Attention seekers perform outlandish stunts for clicks and cash, such as lighting firecrackers on foreheads (or under groins), quaffing down bottles of high-strength *baijiu* or, in the case of one foolhardy foodie in Sichuan, downing a full glass of super-spicy chili oil (he ended up in hospital with severe tonsillitis and a stomach abscess for his troubles).

For less adventurous types, Kuaishou offers a chance to showcase real talent on a platform they can not only control, but directly profit from (fans show their appreciation to the performer by donating virtual gifts such as beer, flowers, and fancy cars; these can be converted to real currency, with the proceeds split equally between the recipient and the platform). There are decent earners like Qi Zhi'ang from Liaoning province, who posts videos playing guitar while his mother sings; the 17-year-old easily makes around 20,000 RMB a month from his 65 million paying fans. Or more modest moneymakers like Tangshan taxi driver Zhao

In his studio, producer Dai Rui still performs shows for old times' sake and to keep his fans happy

Xinlong, who moonlights as Zhao Long'er, nighttime raconteur, cracking ribald jokes to around 100,000 viewers who, together with advertisements for health products and Vietnamese "gold," make him a much-needed extra 6,000 RMB a month, according to The Economist.

And then there are the major players—the *wanghong* (网红, "web celebrities"). MC Brother Li dropped out of school at 15 to become a mechanic; the 30-year-old now makes 1 to 1.5 million RMB (146,000 to 218,000 USD) per month performing *hanmai* (喊麦, "microphone shouting"), loudly rapping over the thumping techno typically found in provincial nightclubs. Aspiring "stream queens" can look to the success of Wen'er, whose energetic chats and *hanmai* performances have earned her 12 million live-streaming app YY followers. Probably hanmai's biggest star, though, is MC Tianyou, a working-class northeasterner with over 17 million YY fans and

Kuaishou is associated with small towns and grassroots acts

a millionaire lifestyle, who raps about the tribulations of growing up poor and dreaming big in small-town China.

Launched in 2011, Kuaishou's extraordinary growth had remained largely under the radar of the metropolitan beltway that dominates China's official media, until the previous year. In January 2016, China Unicom announced that Kuaishou was generating more traffic on its network than mobile behemoths such as messaging app WeChat and microblog platform Weibo. Then in September, a widely-shared article by Huo Qiming, who runs popular WeChat account "doctorx666," entitled "The Brutal Grassroots Phenomenon: A Snapshot of China's Countryside in an App," finally brought Kuaishou under the mainstream microscope.

Huo used the app's most extreme content to make a doom-laden (if familiar) argument about the abject state of China's provincial interior. Rural education is in a state of crisis with dropout rates for secondary school as high as 63 percent, according to the China Agricultural Policy Research Center, Huo observed. Meanwhile, rural-urban migration and the subsequent dissolution of traditional family units have fostered indifferent attitudes toward education and a lack of parental and social guidance among "left-behind" children (one criticism that's hard to refute is the extent of Kuaishou content involving minors that might be considered exploitative or even sexually suggestive).

"A lack of cultural nourishment and the absence of any guardians naturally means children's common contact is with vulgar, brutal things," Huo wrote. "China's villages have been sowing a violent seed." Those who've dropped out or failed their exams find themselves easily drawn to shallow fantasies of making quick money on the internet, Huo claimed—the gospel of mindless "might is right" materialism preached by streaming stars such as MC Tianyou.

Observing their lack of representation in popular culture, Huo pointed to the widening urban-rural divide and vast wealth gap as signs of a country increasingly deaf to the lifestyles of the majority of its citizens, questioning whether anyone considers what the isolated lives of the old and left-behind are like, and concluding: "No one cares."

The regions where Kuaishou is most popular—such as China's manufacturing northeast—have much in common with the Rust Belt communities whose fortunes have declined so precipitously in the US over the last two decades. The massive reforms of state-owned industry in the early 1990s saw vast swathes of redundancies, leaving those who'd grown up with "iron rice bowl" futures in factories with neither jobs nor the know-how to find them. For the children of these laid-off industrial workers, a slowing economy has left them little better off than their parents— official statistics predict an annual GDP growth of 6.7 percent, the country's lowest in decades.

Some parts of the northeast are already in full-blown recession. In 2015, one mining company, the Longmay Group, announced the lay-off of 40 percent of its workforce, affecting 100,000 workers at 42 mines in four cities. The price of coal, the lifeblood of China's industrial heartland, has fallen 60 percent since 2011, according to Shanghai energy consultants ICIS C1 Energy, and strikes and labor protests are on the rise. In former industrial success stories like Shenyang, smoggy capital of Liaoning province, growth has slowed to 3.5 percent amid a housing glut and manufacturing decline. Across provinces like Heilongjiang and Jilin, aging industries like mines and steel mills are shuttering and offering their workers lump-sum payoffs. As a result, hundreds of towns and cities face with bleak prospects for employment or income.

It is in such a hardscrabble culture of suburban frustration and small-town subsistence that Kuaishou's users have grown up. For those without the wealth, connections or education to seek better opportunities, Kuaishou offers a chance to seek out their dreams or demonstrate skills to an audience of millions—a kind of online audition. Self-taught artist and full-time electrician Lu Xiaoyu, for example, managed to secure a number of clients for his 3D drawings and portraits after showcasing them on Kuaishou.

For every success story, however, there are millions more untold failures. And there may be tougher times to come. After years of allowing the live-stream market to flourish unimpeded, the government has stepped in to ensure that its content remain more in tune with "socialist values." There have been clampdowns, as well as arrests for producing pornographic content.

Those who do become celebrities through legitimate forms of entertainment such as *hanmai* face a fate arguably worse than censorship: indifference. Despite receiving tens of thousands of appreciative clicks for each of her streaming videos, *hanmai* singer Wen'er has had little success trying to cross over to mainstream entertainment. In September, she released the original composition "Shengnü Xinjing" ("Heart of a Leftover Woman") on online music platform NetEase Cloud; it garnered just under a hundred comments.

Those who do get attention must also deal with scorn from the elites whose lifestyles they emulate. When GQ magazine profiled MC Tianyou, the backlash from readers was intense: "Disgusting," commented one. Others wondered why the magazine was bothering to promote such a "shady" character, asking, "Why would you even interview this kind of person?"

The future does not look to be getting any easier for China's live-streaming hopefuls. Although many breakout stars say they support the new regulations—for one thing, they thin out the competition—the introduction of requirements for streaming platforms to obtain broadcasting licenses in 2017 is likely to have a knock-on effect on both the diversity and interest in apps such as Kuaishou and their aspiring *wanghong*.

Only the big hitters are expected to survive the impending cull, expert say—and their control of the new media does not bode well for the small-town rookies dreaming of life in the big time. Six Rooms CEO Li Yan, for example, plans to use algorithms and big data to calculate which facets of live streamers are most lucrative—looks, accent, style—and search for performers who fit the "perfect" mould for his app. Live streaming may have started as an upstart revolution against the mainstream, but in the future looks destined to become simply another part of it.

It's Shou Time!

Meet the performers and producers of China's most popular live-streaming app:

The Comedian

Zhou Qianbai is a 20-year-old striver from Hulin, a small city in Heilongjiang province with a single main street and little in the way of entertainment for men his age. Zhou dropped out of school at 15 and moved southward to balmy Guangdong, where he trained in martial arts, hoping to find work as an actor. Lonely and homesick, and having found little in the way of success down south, Zhou returned home in 2014. It was in Hulin, where he now lives with his mother, that he turned to Kuaishou as an outlet for his skills.

The app allows Zhou to indulge in his own ideas for sketches and comedy videos. By sharing these clips, Zhou has attracted around 30,000 followers to date. In the recession-hit economy of northeast China, it's difficult for young people to find a high-earning job; nor can they earn a living simply by broadcasting. Zhou teaches martial arts to kids to help make ends meet. Few believe he is going to become web celebrity like the iconic MC Tianyou, least of all his girlfriend, Jing, 23, who runs a private kindergarten outside Hulin, and doesn't like or understand his enthusiasm for Kuaishou. She would rather Zhou be a "traditional, caring man" with a reliable job, who dedicates all his free time to her; it's a constant source of contention for the couple.

But that doesn't stop Zhou from dreaming. After his parents divorced, his father remarried. Although the two still see each

Zhou shoots a new video in a teahouse opened by his friend. Most of Zhou's videos feature Zhou with his Hulin friends. In this scene, he is pretending to be the the wealthy owner of the shop

Zhou and friends at a nightclub in Hulin

1. Meiko uses a professional studio to broadcast her live shows. Companies are springing up all over China to provide working spaces for aspiring Kuaishou celebrities

2. Zhang displays her work during a broadcast. Many of Zhang's followers are amateur artists who use her videos for tips on improving their own work

3. Studio systems like Dai's give amateur acts a chance to shine professionally

4. Dai, who once made thousands of RMB for his performances, now prefers the corporate life, managing others in his agency

other, Zhou feels his father never really cared about him and looks down on what he does. "If I get rich and famous in the future, I want to buy a big new house for my mother, to thank her for supporting what I'm trying to do," says Zhou.

Although Zhou can earn up to 300 RMB for one of his daily broadcasts, he knows that this is not a sustainable future. Under pressure from his girlfriend, Zhou eventually decided to borrow 20,000 RMB to start his own kung fu class at his girlfriend's school, teaching students aged 6 to 15, whose parents pay him 300 RMB a month. With his weekends spent teaching, Zhou has put his Kuaishou ambitions on hold in order to keep faith with his family—he still makes videos, only these ones promote his new business, rather than his true passion for comedy.

The Painter

An art major at Shenyang Ligong University, Zhang Ciman, 22, also helps run a coffee shop in Shenyang where she began her modest broadcasting career about a year ago. By sharing her artwork and singing songs on request, Zhang has accumulated over 10,000 followers. Hundreds of these fans watch her live shows every day, and Zhang uses the virtual gifts from her audience to help pay off tuition fees of around 5,000 RMB per semester, as well as living expenses.

"My mother knows that I'm involved in broadcasting. She even watches my show and helps me deal with some of the problems I have during the performance," Zhang says. "By earning money, I feel I am more independent."

The Anchors

Zhao Pengbo, 23, has just graduated from the Beijing University of Aeronautics and Astronautics, where he studied to be a flight attendant. Unlike his classmates, Zhao has no immediate plans to start a career which, while seeming glamorous—especially to those who haven't traveled abroad—can be difficult to advance within. Instead, Zhao has decided to see if he can use his natural charm to make a living as a "cyber anchor," broadcasting himself singing and chatting with fans. He tapes live shows in a special recording room for three hours day, earning around 5,000 RMB a month.

"It's a trend and fashionable for young people to try [online broadcasting]. Nowadays the market is growing rapidly," says Zhao. "I like it because this job is more flexible. I can have time and space for myself after work. My parents think it's not real work...[but] I don't care."

Fellow anchor Meiko, also from Shenyang, was working as a sales assistant and gym instructor before she discovered Kuaishou and decided she had what it takes to host her own show. She has joined a production company for live streamers, which has hired about 30 young anchors, mainly female, and provides them with broadcasting equipment and a recording studio. Other than a basic salary of around 2,000 RMB, a top anchor can earn around 20,000 to 50,0000 RMB a month, mainly via payment from their fans, so their survival is dependent on popularity and consistent updates.

The Singer-Turned-Producer

Dai Rui is holding court to his fans at his office in Liaoyang, Liaoning province. Just 24, Dai is already a successful entrepreneur and producer of professional live-streaming shows, but he was once an ordinary online performer, like his employees.

Dai first broke into the business in 2014, and his enthusiastic singing soon earned him a massive following. His fans included several rich businessmen who were willing to give him expensive gifts for his performances—soon his income reached as much as 200,000 RMB a month (wealthy users are often motivated to donate large amounts as a show of face; sometimes they even compete to be a performer's most generous patron).

The income allowed Dai to break out of the performer's life and become his own producer. The Liaoyang Zhiyuan Culture and Communication Company now turns over several million RMB a year, and Dai has more than a thousand streaming singers on contract.

But despite the wealth and acclaim it brought him, Dai doesn't miss his singing days. "The broadcasting industry made me successful, it also ruined my normal life," Dai recalls. "I used to broadcast more than 15 hours a day. It hurt my body badly. Now I have more money than I could imagine, but I still don't have enough time. If I could do it again, I may not choose to broadcast." - Wu Hao (吴皓)

Originally published in May 2017

Thinking Inside the Box

Black box theater and Chinese opera:
what's not to like?

The iridescent opera costumes are opulent against the backdrop of black box theater, yet at times, at the lower registers especially, you lose the words sung on the cavernous stage. Such are the lessons of Star Theater's third annual Xiqu Opera Black Box Festival in Beijing: In the formidable undertaking of making contemporary adaptations to millennia-old Chinese art forms, you win some and lose some.

The festival, which runs from October to the end of December 2016, gives the Chinese translation for "black box" as, literally, "small theater" (小剧场). It's not exactly accurate, since black box theater primarily tends to be defined not by size as much as by an unadorned, streamlined look and flexible use of space, as the arrangement of the seats are not fixed and can be changed as needed. In this year's festival, 17 out of the 19 official selections played in Star Theater's two biggest auditoriums, boasting more than plush 200 seats each, with an audience seated on one side as with the traditional proscenium stage.

In this case, explains Hu Hanchi, a student director whose work was featured in this year's festival, black box or "small theater" ought to be interpreted in a relative sense. "It's not the space getting smaller, people getting fewer, but it refers to a closeness of performers to the audience," he says. "It's about getting close enough to see what the creator wants to express." At the Xiqu Opera Festival, this comes of playing directly on the auditorium floor, using minimal sets and technical distractions, and by creatively reimagining of the boundaries of the stage—including emotional boundaries.

Billed as an "experimental Kunqu opera" by the festival organizers, Hu's work, *Three Incarnations* (《三生》), is based on a story of the same name from Pu Songling's *Strange Tales from a Chinese Studio* (《聊斋志异》). In this tale, a man is able to recall three of his past lives—as a district magistrate, a dog, and an official overseeing the civil service examination—and his conflict with the same reincarnated adversary in each life.

In terms of its themes and presentation, Hu's piece holds perhaps the middle ground among the festival's selected works. The official selection ran the gamut of ancient theatrical and operatic works garnished with a few lines of modern vernacular for comic effect to full postmodern pastiches, where traditional operatic themes are just some of the many cultural elements that appear alongside hip hop, internet slang, and belly dance.

For Hu, *Three Incarnations* was ideal meat for black box theater, being a work with an introspective theme and extremely limited cast. As a matter of fact, he is his opera's the only performer, as well as its director and one of its two writers. His is also one of

Some of the works performed at the festival are updated with
humorous interludes and asides in modern spoken Chinese

only two works at this year's festival (along with a children's
opera) that played in a small auditorium with a "fan-shaped"
stage, which has the audience seated on three sides and allows
greater freedom with the performers' use of direction and space.
By changing the original story's three past lives to horse, dog,
and snake, Hu allows himself to make more innovative use of
body movements—honed by years of punishingly comprehensive
studies at the National Academy of Chinese Theatre Arts—as
well as reimagine the function of stock opera roles *sheng, dan*, and
chou as being analogous of the three lives in the story, suggesting
a coexistence of different moral qualities in one person when all
played by the single actor.

The rest of the Xiqu Opera Festival's programming is a mix of
adaptations to traditional works in the major operatic genres of
Peking, Kunqu, Yue (Shaoxing), Gan, and Yue (Canton) genres,

The opera *Two Belles in Love* reinterprets Qing dramatist Li Yu's *The Fragment Companion* as a love story between the two female leads as well as more imaginative oeuvres such as a Chinese opera-infused take on Shakespeare's *As You Like It* and a performance of *ache lhamo*, sometimes called "Tibetan musical theater." There is also the closing performance, *Four Westward Dreams*, an original production (very) loosely inspired by the works of sixteenth century playwright Tang Xianzu (汤显祖)—*all* of his works.

In this last production, the festival somewhat falters. Opera influences are woven with fanatical care into the actors' every movement and sustained note of their voice; the action primarily consists of pop culture-infused dialogue and dance numbers that are meant to take audiences out of the action and mirror the jarring, absurd changes of scenery and mood that they experience while dreaming.

They succeed all too well: eating up any attention the audience might give to the actors' technical finesse and the play's occasionally breathtaking visual tableaux, which are the typical takeaways of a Chinese opera performance and shown off to special advantage by the minimalist black box setting. As two students in the audience complained afterwards, "it was just a regular play"—and not one that had the stealthiest references or that advanced any sort of biting critique with its pastiche and parody.

The road to modernizing Chinese opera, to be fair, was never going to be easy. Throughout modern Chinese history, each generation has tried to reinterpret opera according to what were deemed to be the fundamental political and moral values of their era. In the Republic of China period, the art developed codified techniques, training schools, and classic repertoire in reflection of a society-wide push toward more "scientific" ways of practicing culture; purists then protested, citing how the old (and famously brutal) training system produced elite performers unmatched in level of skill and dedication to the craft. The infamous "Eight Model Operas" sanctioned during the Cultural Revolution were later repudiated for monotony and overt political messages, pushed at the expense of artistic merit.

Black box, on the other hand, is a somewhat recent phenomenon, appearing in China for the first time in 1995. It is primarily associated with youth directors and audiences and cultivates a decidedly niche identity. It's still much easier to find listing for performances on social media than major magazines and city entertainment guides, while the venues tend to cluster around art districts and, increasingly, commercial areas catering to "artistic youths." According to Hu, the black box concept is only beginning to take hold in the world of opera, but, like all contemporary movements, it's nothing more than an invitation to express the ideas of contemporary society.

"As a post-90s generation creator I want to honor the ancient heritage of opera, but I also personally feel like opera can be 'cool,' so my production company and I like to express our work that way," he says. "On the other hand, traditional opera format is too immensely rich and complex, so our challenge was to adapt it fit the unusual themes of the story in order to express our iconoclastic personality."

"The word 'experimental,' is not something I came up with, but a label the festival gave my show—but similarly, I feel like that's all relative, that any creation is an experiment and any opera in a 'small theater' is already experimental," Hu says. - Hatty Liu

Originally published in January 2017